FOREWORD

IN one form or another we have heard the expression similar to this: " It is an object lesson which we may well take to heart." An object lesson is so called because the lesson is derived from something tangible, something we can see. The oral lesson makes its appeal primarily to the mind and from there must be transmitted into life and not until then does it become an experiment in living. But the object lesson, although it appeals to the mind, is an experiment from the beginning. Experimenting with great truths has a greater appeal than theorizing about them. Especially is this true of Junior age children who are extremely practical and very impatient with theorizing. Demonstrate a truth to a child and he is more easily convinced.

We can see, therefore, that an object lesson is always much more impressive and lasting than an oral lesson. The use of objects which are familiar to the children is, therefore, a very effective way of teaching spiritual truths. Most children of the Junior age are from " Missouri "; they want to be shown. A wise teacher of religion will cater to the prevailing wholesome emotions and attitudes in the pupils for the transmitting of moral and spiritual truths. With that in mind this book of Junior Object Sermons was written.

J. J. S.

JUNIOR OBJECT SERMONS

JUNIOR OBJECT SERMONS

By
J. J. SESSLER

BAKER BOOK HOUSE
Grand Rapids, Michigan

Reprinted 1968 by
Baker Book House Company

ISBN: 0-8010-7937-3

First printing, August 1968
Second printing, September 1969
Third printing, February 1972

PHOTOLITHOPRINTED BY CUSHING - MALLOY, INC.
ANN ARBOR, MICHIGAN, UNITED STATES OF AMERICA
1972

CONTENTS

1

THE SALT OF THE EARTH

Object: Salt.

Story: Christ said to His followers, " Ye are the salt of the earth." When we look at this salt we say to ourselves, " I don't look like that." But we shall see. A Roman proverb states that sunlight and salt are the two things which keep the world alive and sweet. From the very beginning of history men have set a high value on salt. A bag of salt among barbarians was worth more than a man. The ancient Germans gathered for worship in the salt districts and considered them the proper places to build their temples.

In the eastern countries salt is a symbol of friendship. To eat salt with another man was to accept his friendship. In Abyssinia and Tibet cakes of salt are used for money. The Jews considered salt of great value because they lived in a hot climate where it was absolutely essential to keep their food from spoiling. In Palestine they even salted the new-born babies. This was done by rubbing the baby with salt and olive oil and then wrapping bands of cloth around it until it looked like a mummy. These bands remained on the child from seven to forty days as a protection against infection. Then, in the days of Augustine, at the time of a baby's baptism, a little pinch of salt was put on its tongue as a symbol of purity.

Throughout the ages people, therefore, have put a high value on this common salt. When Jesus said,

" Ye are the salt of the earth," He had a very definite meaning in His mind.

Salt is used to season food. Just think of trying to eat a meal without salt. I can see you make faces. An Irish boy said, " Salt is the thing which if you don't put it in 'taters, they ain't good." A king asked his three daughters how much they loved him. Two replied that they loved him better than silver or gold, but the third said, " Father, I love you better than salt." The king was very angry at such a comparison. But the cook, who overheard the remark, left the salt out of the king's breakfast. Then the king understood that his daughter loved him so well that nothing was good without him.

Salt, then, adds taste and flavor to all that it touches. If it has been omitted from a food we know what is wrong at once. The religion of Jesus is a way to make life taste good. Our job as followers of Jesus is to take our religion and use it to add tang and flavor to our lives. If we are generous, willing to share, more neighborly, and through our cheerfulness encourage others, we are salt. We are seasoning our own lives and the lives of others.

Salt penetrates food very quickly. Put some in a glass of water and the water soon tastes salty. We, like salt, should have this quality. We can use our influence for good on others.

One morning, after a three days' rain, everyone in the house felt cross. The baby was crying, the fire was smoking, and the breakfast room was gloomy. Then Jack came in. He handed the morning paper to his father, saying cheerfully, " Good news today, father." Then he kissed his mother and had a bright word and smile for his little sister. He then poked the fire, making several amusing remarks. Soon everyone had forgotten all about the weather. Jack had completely changed the atmosphere with his happy, sunny influence. He was the salt, he scattered a grain here, another one there, and soon everyone was seasoned just right.

Salt also preserves. It keeps the living from dying. Everyone needs it. Normally, a man uses a peck of salt a year. Without salt a pigeon can live only three months and a dog only six months. Lieutenant Herndon says that in crossing South America his cattle and horses died of starvation, even while they were eating the rich green grass, because his supply of salt had become exhausted. Thus we can see that salt is very essential to human life. Neither man nor beast can live without salt. When Jesus said that we should be like salt, He meant to say that Christians are as necessary to the world as salt is for men and animals.

Salt is powerful. What a foolish remark to make! How can these grains of salt be powerful? They can lift objects if enough of them are added to water. The Dead Sea, which contains four times as much salt as the ocean, will easily float an egg or bear up the weight of a man enough to keep him from drowning. You see, the salt lifts, it has lifting power. As salt, we, too, must have that effect on others. When we cut a finger, all the throw-off of salt in perspiration or other ways from our bodies stops. The salt in us is called to the wounded place to help ward off blood-poisoning.

When we all work together, we become powerful. When the grains of salt unite in the water, they can lift. So we, as salt, must use our seasoning, penetrating, preserving and lifting qualities to make this world a better place in which to live.

2

WHAT GOLD CANNOT BUY

Object: A piece of gold jewelry.

Story: " Gold buys everything." The speaker was one of the village wise men. The place was the grocery store. The grocer, who was old and stooped, looked over the top of his spectacles, smiled, and said, " Yes, gold buys everything, everything but three things— health, happiness, and heaven." I wonder whether he was right? Shall we try to figure this out for ourselves?

Already, in the second chapter of Genesis, we find mention of gold, of which this chain is made. And from then until now men have been eager to find it.

Two German brothers came to America in 1845. The older brother, who was experienced in the making of sauerkraut, bought a farm in California in order to raise cabbages. The younger brother stayed in New York and learned the science of metallurgy. Later, the younger brother went to California to visit his older brother. The latter took his younger brother on a tour of inspection over the farm. The younger brother paid no attention to the cabbages, but continually examined the soil and rock on the farm. Finally, he pointed to a dull yellow metallic spot on a rock, and said, " Brother, that is gold. You have been growing your cabbage heads on a gold mine." Thousands of people rushed to California when they heard of the discovery of gold. It caused much exictement. All hoped for speedy wealth. Many failed, and only a few succeeded in their search.

Why are people so anxious for gold? (Again hold up jewelry.) Since early times, it has been thought of as the rarest and the most precious of all metals. It is beautiful, bright and glistening. It is durable. Other metals rust, decay, or are eaten by acid, but gold always remains the same. It is the chief means of exchange between buyers and sellers. Gold will buy everything you eat, drink, or wear. If we have plenty of it we will have power to buy everything.

Everything, did I say? Many people have the idea that gold will buy happiness. One of these was King Midas. According to the fairy story, he was so greedy for gold that he asked the gods for the power to turn everything he touched into gold. His wish was granted. One morning when he awoke he found that he possessed the longed-for gift. When he touched his bed and table, both became solid gold. He went around touching the ornaments and the flowers, which also became gold. His heart was filled with joy. He thought to himself, " Now I am the happiest man on earth." Just then his little daughter whom he loved dearly came into the room. He bent over and kissed her. She became a lifeless statue of gold. Was he now the happiest man on earth? The high value he had placed on gold had made him the most miserable man that ever lived. We do not need gold in order to be happy. We can never buy happiness with gold. Happiness is something that is in the heart and has nothing to do with gold.

The grocer also said that health was of more value than gold. Do you remember in the story, " The Bird's Christmas Carol," that Carol was a rich girl who was very sick? Next door lived a large poor family in which all the children were very healthy. With all

Carol's wealth, no doctor could cure her. How happy health would have made her! She would gladly have been poor and healthy like her neighbors. Be happy, be content that God has given you a healthy body, which is of more value than much gold.

Heaven, too, is of more value than gold. (Hold up jewelry.) By heaven we mean God and all that is pure, good and holy. It is said that hunters catch monkeys by making a hole in a keg and putting some sugar in it. The monkey, anxious to get the sugar, puts his hand into the hole and fills his fist with sugar. When he sees the hunter coming he wants to withdraw his hand, but the closed fist filled with sugar cannot be withdrawn. Rather than drop the sugar, the silly creature allows himself to be captured. He sacrifices his liberty for the price of a handful of sugar.

Jesus told of a very rich man who loved his gold more than heaven. Like the monkey who had his fist full of sugar and would not let go of it, so this rich man had his fists full of gold. He believed his gold was worth more than heaven. That night he died, and he missed heaven.

Let us remember that gold can buy many things, but it cannot buy health, happiness, and heaven.

3

"WHITER THAN SNOW"

Object: A bowl of snow.

Story: A little girl went out to play in the snow and coming in, said, "Mama, I couldn't help praying when I was outside playing."

"What did you pray, my child?" asked the mother.

"I prayed the snow-prayer, Mama, that I learned in Sunday school: 'Wash me, and I shall be whiter than snow.'"

What a wonderful change a snowfall makes in the appearance of the country. We wake up some wintry morning and look out of the windows and see how beautiful everything appears. It seems as if a fairy has been at work. The road, the trees, the ground and the weeds are all covered with a white carpet. The earth looks white and beautiful. No wonder the little girl prayed, "Wash me, and I shall be whiter than snow."

Have you ever examined a snowflake closely? In Jericho, Vermont, lived a man named Wilson Bentley who was called "The Snowflake Man." Studying snowflakes was his hobby. For forty-seven years he made photographs of snowflakes. He took more than five thousand pictures. After a snowstorm he used to say that he had received "a birthday gift from King Winter." Every one of the pictures of the snowflakes was like a perfect crystal and no two were alike. Verily, the snow is beautiful; each crystal is formed by the Great Artist, God.

"But," you ask, "isn't the snow of any use?"

In the Book of Job we read, "For he saith to the snow, fall thou on the earth." Also, "Hast thou entered into the treasures of the snow?" We know that whatever God sends is good and Job tells us that snow is a treasure. So we must delve into the snow in order to understand it.

Snow is a substitute for the sun. Strange, but true. When the cold nights of winter come, your mother spreads warm woolen blankets on your bed to keep you warm. The Bible says, "God sendeth snow like wool."

When the ground is cold and the roots of the plants and grass are in danger of freezing, God spreads a beautiful white comforter of snow over the ground to keep it warm. The farmers will tell us that one of the useful services of snow is to cover the winter wheat to keep it from freezing. But when the sun shines bright and warm, the snow coverlet disappears. It is no longer needed. God is good, He knows that the roots and plants must be kept warm so that our daily bread materializes in the summer.

Looking at this snow, we wonder whether it has still another use. When the snow falls on mountain tops in great quantities, it hardens into glaciers. When this snow melts in the spring, it runs down the mountain sides in little streams and in that way waters and fertilizes the valleys. In some countries where the sun is intensely hot and very little rain falls, nothing would grow if it were not for the melting snow irrigating the land. No man, woman or child could live in a country of that kind, for no life could exist.

The snowflakes that God sends show us that God is wise and that He loves us. Through His wisdom He provides material things for our welfare. With His love He provides for our needs.

The snow is of great benefit in helping to cure some diseases. By living in a cold climate where there is plenty of snow people with tuberculosis usually come back home strong and healthy.

" God saith to the snow, be thou on the earth." The snow arrives in all its beauty. It covers, warms and waters the earth. Only a good, all-wise God could so adequately and in such a beautiful way provide for us.

4

USING THE BEST IN US

Objects: A piece of coal and a piece of coke.

Story: This piece of coal has come to church with me today to preach a sermon. If you think that the only thing for which coal is used is to heat our homes, you are mistaken. Suppose I put this piece of coal into a closed heated oven. Then when I remove it after a short time, it would look like this. (Hold up the piece of coke.) This is a piece of coke. Of course, this coke also is used for heating purposes. However, through this heating process the coal has given off gas and vapors which are very useful. We call them by-products. Just think, from eighty million tons of coal we get about fifty million tons of coke plus $650,000,-000 worth of by-products.

I would like to tell you about one of these by-products which we call coal tar. Coal tar is a black gummy substance; it is a favorite raw material for the chemist. He seems to be able to get all sorts of things from it. He makes dyes, perfumes, spot removers, drugs, fertilizers, plastics, and explosives. From the one compound he gets a whole rainbow of dyes; saccharine, which is three hundred times as sweet as sugar; perfume, TNT explosive, aspirin, which many people use for headaches; disinfectants, such as lysol; coumarin, which is used in place of vanilla; a water-proofing substance used in the concrete to keep water out of cellars, and dynamite and poison gas.

All these things which I have mentioned are in this piece of coal. One would never think so just by look-

ing at it. Now you can see how useful is the coal which
God has put deep into the earth for the use of man.
There are materials in this coal which can be used for
good or evil. Drugs to cure the sick, explosives to be
made into bombs to kill people in war. Poison gas to
spread destruction and dyes of rainbow hue such as we
have in our clothes.   However, all these products can
be a help to us.   For instance, the explosives can be
used to remove obstacles in the way of building a good
highway and the poison gas can be used to eliminate
harmful insects.

We are just like this piece of coal. In us are all
kinds of powers and abilities which can be used for
good or bad, for right or wrong.

One such power I'd like to mention is " determination."   One evening Joe's mother called to him, " Joe,
it's time to do your home work." Joe replied, " I don't
like to study. I won't work tonight." Joe was determined not to work.   Bill, another boy of my acquaint-
ance, was on his way to school.   Suddenly he heard a
call, " Come on, Bill, let's play hookey today." Bill,
however, could not be persuaded to miss school; he
was determined to go to his classes. Both Bill and Joe
had the trait of determination; the difference was that
Bill used it in the right way and Joe in the wrong way.
Determination in us, just like the by-products in coal,
can be used for good or evil.

About two thousand years ago there was born in the
city of Tarsus a boy who was named Saul. He received
a good education, studying to be a rabbi, a Jewish
teacher. At this time Jesus was living in Judea. Many
people believed that He was the Savior.   These followers of His were called Christians. Saul, like the
majority of the Jewish leaders, thought that Jesus was

an impostor and therefore was of the opinion that the teachings of Jesus should be stamped out. So Saul became very zealous in the persecution of the Christians. One day he was on his way to the city of Damascus, having heard that he would find there many Christian leaders, whom he determined to destroy. However, before he arrived, he had a vision, in which he heard the voice of Jesus saying, " Saul, Saul, why persecutest thou me? " Convinced against his will that Jesus was the Christ, he used all his talents and all his zeal to further the cause of Christianity in the world. In fact, he became the first Christian missionary traveling to every country of the then known world. Saul became known as Paul. He used the same talents for Christ which he had formerly used against Him. He used his great ability for good instead of evil.

So we too, like Paul, must do our best to use our strength and ability in the right way. Let us remember that what is in this coal can be used for good or evil. In the same way the strength and abilities we have can be used for good or bad. We all know that they should be used to do good.

5

THANKSGIVING

Objects: A loaf of bread and a kernel of wheat.

Story: Here, in my left hand I hold a kernel of wheat; in my right hand I have a loaf of bread, and since Thursday is Thanksgiving, I ought to tell you something about thankfulness. I wonder what the kernel of wheat and the loaf of bread have in common with Thanksgiving. When we go to the bakery to buy the bread, is that reason enough to be thankful? However, let us pause for a moment and think. In my mind flashes the story of Charles and his dream.

Charles' parents were poor; often they had very little to eat. One day they had for lunch just a loaf of bread like the one in my hand.

Charles said, " Mother, is that all we are having for lunch? I want some butter and strawberry jam, too."

" I am sorry," mother answered, " but I have no butter and jam for you. We ought to be thankful for this loaf of bread."

" I am going up to my room," said Charles. " I don't want any bread. I see no reason to be thankful for an old loaf of bread."

Charles left the table, went to his room, and lay down on his bed disgruntled. He fell asleep. In his dream he heard the loaf of bread say to him, " Charles, follow me, and I will show you why you ought to be thankful for me."

First, they went to the bakery. " Mr. Baker," said the loaf of bread, " Charles wants to know why he ought to be thankful for me."

" Oh, loaf of bread, I could tell Charles, but I feel as if he should find out for himself," answered the baker. " I have made many loaves like you and I buy the wheat flour of which you are made from the miller. Why don't you ask him? "

So the two, Charles and the loaf of bread, went on. Soon they came to the mill. " Mr. Miller," said the loaf of bread, " I asked the baker why Charles should be thankful for me and he sent me to you. Can you help me with my problem? "

" Yes, I can help you, but Charles ought to discover the reason for himself," said the miller. " You see, I grind the wheat into flour. You must seek further. Go to the farmer, he's the one that brings me the wheat."

So Charles and the loaf of bread continued on their way into the country. They finally arrived at the farm. " Mr. Farmer," said the loaf of bread, " Charles wants to know why he should be thankful for me. We asked the baker this same question; he sent us to the miller and the miller sent us to you."

" Come with me," said the farmer. So he took the two to the granary, which was filled with kernels of wheat. " These are the kernels of wheat (show kernel which you are holding in your left hand) which I take to the mill," said the farmer. " Charles, I wonder whether you can tell me where I get these kernels."

" Yes," answered Charles, " they grow."

" You are right," answered the farmer, " but what makes them grow? "

Charles thought for a moment and then answered, " The sun and the rain cause them to grow."

" Correct," said the farmer, " but who sends the sunshine and the rain? "

" God sends them," answered Charles.

" That is right," replied the farmer, " and that is the real reason for being thankful to God for a loaf of bread. God makes the wheat grow. I only plant the seed and harvest the crop. The miller merely grinds the wheat into flour and the baker makes the flour into a loaf of bread. Yes, God is the one who gives us the wheat. The baker, the miller, and I are His helpers."

Then Charles awoke. The dream was very real and had taught him a lesson. " Mother," he said, " I am sorry that I was so cross this noon. I had a wonderful dream which taught me a lesson of true thankfulness. I do thank God for this loaf of bread."

The first Thanksgiving in our country was celebrated by the Pilgrims. They did not thank God for great quantities of food. They were thankful for a loaf of bread, for being alive, for having lived through a long, cold winter and thankful that God had been with them.

We need to thank God not only for food, warm clothing, homes and our parents, but for two eyes which can see the beauty of God's world, two ears to hear the voice of God, two hands to work for Him and a mouth to tell others about Him. Truly, this ought to be a thankful Thanksgiving for us.

6

SEEING OURSELVES

Object: A mirror.

Story: When I look into this mirror, what do I see? Do I hear someone say, " Yourself " ? Yes, I see myself, as others see me. I would like to tell you the story of Priscilla, who lived many years ago, during pioneer days. Priscilla's home was in New England. One day her father decided to move further west, where he could have a large farm. So, in a covered wagon, Priscilla and her parents started out. They planned to settle in Iowa, about twelve hundred miles away; therefore, it would take months to reach their destination. After about a week of travel, Priscilla started to get careless about her appearance. When they stopped for the night, she was too lazy to go after water to wash her face, too indifferent to mend the rips in her clothes, and she just did not feel like combing her hair. By the end of the second week, her mother remonstrated with her, but Priscilla answered angrily, " What's the difference how I look? No one sees me, except you and father. Who cares? " As the days went on, Priscilla's face became dirtier, her hair stringier, and her clothes more ragged. Her mother did not know what to do with her. She wished she had a mirror, but they had none in the covered wagon. But one day the mother sent Priscilla to the pool to fetch some water for cooking. It was just sunset, and the golden glow of the sun was reflected in the clear water of the pool.

As Priscilla bent down, pail in hand, she saw a terrifying face mirrored in the pool—cheeks streaked with dirt, unkempt, stringy hair, and forehead creased with a frown. Who could that untidy, frowning creature be? Suddenly, just when I glance into this mirror and see myself as others see me, so Priscilla saw herself as she really was. She touched her face, then her hair, and then the frowning lines on her forehead, and burst into tears. " Why, oh why did I do this to myself? " she sobbed. " No wonder mother protests to me every day. I did not know I looked so badly. From now on I will keep myself neat and tidy."

Priscilla finally saw herself as others saw her. Whenever that happens to anyone, there is always a change for the better. Other people see our faces and whether we keep our clothes clean, and they see more than our faces and our clothes. There is one who sees even more than that. He is God. If we could only see ourselves as God sees us.

How do you think we look to God when we are not pure and clean in our hearts? God looks right into our hearts. How do we look when we are terribly angry? If you should ever be very angry again, run to a mirror and look at yourself. What a face! That is the way others see you, and, what is still worse, God sees you that way. Not a very nice face to look at, is it? Then smile into the mirror and see what an improvement that is. See yourself smiling. When you smile, that is the way others see you, and what is best of all, God sees you that way.

Are you selfish at times? Are you afraid that others will have a little more than you have? When there is a big apple and a small one, do you grab the big one and leave the small one for your friend? That is self-ishness. A selfish person is not liked by anyone. Once there was an old miser named Silas Marner. He was very selfish, and his only thought was to get more and more money. Everyone saw him as a selfish old miser, and that is the way God saw him. He lived all alone and no one ever came to visit him. Then one day he saw himself as others saw him. It was not a very nice picture which he saw of himself. He decided to change. He became interested in other people and tried to help wherever he could. He was no longer a miser. What a fine old man he became. Everyone noticed the change. Friends were glad to see him. Silas Marner had become a different man. Others saw him now, not selfish, but generous, and that is the way God saw him.

Yes, a mirror is a great thing. In it we can see our faces as others see them. But God sees our hearts. Do we see ourselves as God sees us? I am certain that we all want our hearts to be as God wants them to be.

7

IN UNITY THERE IS STRENGTH

Object: Toothpicks.

Story: "United we stand, divided we fall." What does this proverb have in common with toothpicks? Let us see how strong one toothpick alone is. How easily it is broken. Now, let us take a bunch of toothpicks. I will try to break them. But, no, it is impossible for me to do so. So the toothpicks and the proverb do have something in common. "United we stand." See, the entire bunch of toothpicks is strong. Now, "divided we fall"—the one toothpick alone was easily broken. So we have proved the truth of the proverb, "United we stand, divided we fall," have we not?

One evening we were sitting before the fireplace watching the glowing coals in the fire. Suddenly one coal tumbled out of the fire onto the hearth. We watched it for a few seconds, and the coal grew dark and cold. An instant before it was alive, giving warmth and light; but when it left the other coals, it became black and soon died. Only when the coals are together do we have a fire. Alone and separated, the hot coals die out. "United we stand, divided we fall."

Our country, called the United States, is another good illustration of our proverb. Suppose that long ago, before the Revolutionary War, each colony or province in this country had stood alone instead of uniting as one. If this had been the case, our beloved country would not have won its freedom. But the thirteen colonies united as one to face a common foe and were victorious. " United we stand." Remember, a bunch of toothpicks is stronger than one lonely toothpick.

One day I heard much argument on the playground. John said, " I want to play marbles." George suggested, " Let's play baseball." Philip whined, " I don't like to play anything but football." Joseph answered, " Well, boys, we're not getting anywhere; John alone cannot play marbles; certainly George cannot play baseball with himself; and Philip cannot play every position in football all alone. So I suggest that we play together, one day marbles, the next baseball, and so on." The boys all liked Joseph's idea and played together. United, they had a good time playing together; divided, there could have been no play.

What is a church? It is a group of people united in worshiping God. Why do so many people stay away from church on Sundays? One says, " I like to worship God alone in the woods." Another suggests, " When I am working alone in my garden, I can best pray to God." A third says, " I like to be alone at the seashore to think about the goodness of God." However, when these people are in the woods, the garden or at the seaside, there are so many things to do and see that they forget all about God. Suppose that these people had all set aside an hour on Sunday morning to meet together in the house of God. United in prayer, they would have received new strength, strength to go on with their everyday work. For Jesus said, " Where two or three are gathered in my name, there am I in their midst." When we all worship God together on Sundays we are united. How easy it is to break one toothpick, but a bunch of toothpicks cannot be so easily broken. So we Christian boys and girls must work together, for " united we stand, divided we fall."

8

WE CAN BE STRONG

Objects: A bullet and a piece of straw.

Story: Do you know what this object is which I hold in my hand? It is a bullet. If I should drop it on the floor, it would roll a short distance and then stop. Even a piece of paper or cardboard would stop it. What would happen, however, if I should fire it from a high-powered gun? It could plow right through a board, could penetrate the trunk of a tree, or shatter a pane of glass. Have you ever heard of a cyclone or a tornado? They are terrific windstorms. Some years ago a tornado raged in Iowa. After the storm was over I saw a piece of straw which the wind had driven into a heavy plank. How weak is a bullet or a straw when left to itself. But how strong is the bullet when powered by a gun or a straw when driven by a storm.

Today we are going to choose a text for our story. It is found in the New Testament, in the Book of Philippians, chapter four, verse thirteen, "I can do all things through Christ which strengtheneth me." These are the words of the Apostle Paul. They have helped and encouraged people ever since.

During our Revolutionary War, when George Washington was the leader of our army, the winter headquarters for the soldiers was at Valley Forge in Pennsylvania. The weather was bitterly cold. The men had very little warm clothing, many had no shoes, and food was scarce. Everyone was discouraged. When the hopes of everyone were at the lowest point, one of the soldiers discovered their leader, George Washington, on his knees in the snow, asking God for help and strength to go on. New courage was given them from above, new power to go on to final victory. George Washington needed the strength of God to give him courage to go on, just as this bullet needs a gun to have power to be of use.

In the Old Testament we read that one of the leaders of Israel was Joshua. He was discouraged with the tremendous task of conquering the land of Canaan with his small untrained army. He asked God for strength to go on, and God said, " Be strong and of good courage. As I have been with Moses, so I will be with thee. Be not discouraged or dismayed. Go forward." Joshua, feeling this nearness of God, went on with great power, and won Canaan for Israel. One man and a small army, strengthened with power from God, became invincible, just as a straw driven by the force of a tornado is very powerful.

As George Washington and Joshua needed the strength and power of God to give them courage to go on, so we, too, need this power in our everyday living. Often, as we study our lessons, we come to a problem which seems unworkable. Just pause for a moment, close your eyes, and say, " O God, I have tried so hard, but it seems impossible for me to solve it." Then you will hear a gentle voice saying, " Try once more, my child." You open your eyes, you find that new courage has been given to you, and soon the seemingly impossible has been accomplished.

The bullet needed the gun, the straw, the storm, but George Washington and Joshua needed the power from above. And we need it. So we must say with Paul, " I can do all things through Christ which strengtheneth me."

9

CORRECTING OUR MISTAKES

Object: An eraser.

Story: In my hand I hold an eraser. With it I erase or rub out. I do not rub out correctly written words but wrong and misspelled ones. Yes, I erase any errors or mistakes which I have made. I try to make my sentence look perfect, as if I had made no error. I correct my mistakes by the use of this eraser.

Do we only make mistakes or errors in writing? Let us look in the Bible and see whether other errors can be made. This time we will look into the Old Testament, in the Book of Jeremiah. One day Jeremiah went to the potter's house. A potter is a man who molds vases or bowls out of clay, and the instrument he uses is called a potter's wheel. When Jeremiah arrived, the potter was molding a vase from clay on the wheel. But the vessel he made was marred, was not perfect. So he used the very same clay and made a new vessel, a perfect one. Just as we correct our mistakes with an eraser and then insert a new word, so the potter removes his mar or mistake by making the clay over into a new vessel.

Now let us turn to the New Testament. You all know that Jesus had twelve disciples, twelve men who followed Him. On the night that Jesus was taken prisoner, wrongfully accused, all His disciples were afraid and left Him. Peter, one of the twelve, was accused three times that night of being a follower of Jesus. And three times he swore that he had never even heard of Jesus. Later, Peter realized how wrong he had been and wept bitterly. Jesus gladly forgave Peter, for He knew that he was truly sorry. But Peter was not only sorry; he felt that he must make this great wrong right. The way to undo a wrong is to erase it and put something good in its place, just as we erase a wrong word with this eraser and put the right word in its place. Everywhere Peter went he told people about Jesus, and fifty days after the death of Jesus he preached to thousands of people and won three thousand new followers.

As Peter corrected this wrong in his life, so we must always correct our mistakes. What kind of mistakes are we making? Have we told a lie and never admitted it? If so, let us take our eraser, erase that lie and tell the truth. Have we been too lazy to study? Then let us erase our laziness and substitute "busyness." Have we been mean to our little brother or sister? With an eraser meanness can be changed to kindness. If we always tell the truth, are busy and kind, we do not need an eraser. But we must remember that the "eraser" is always there, waiting to erase all our mistakes.

10

PURE IN HEART

Objects: Two cups, one clean, inside and outside; the other clean on the outside but dirty on the inside.

Story: Here stand two nice, clean cups. Clean, did I say? Yes, clean on the outside. But now let us look on the inside. This one is clean inside and outside, but look at this other one. It is dirty, very dirty on the inside, although clean on the outside. We certainly could not use this cup unless we thoroughly cleaned it. I wonder what these two cups remind us of. Let us all put on our " thinking caps."

Some years ago there was trouble in a coal mine. The miners were so angry that they set fire to some coal cars and sent them rolling into a tunnel. They started a fire in the mine, which was soon out of control. For weeks it raged underground, undermining roads, buildings, and even entire villages. Suddenly, without any warning, a road would cave in and a building would collapse. The fire burned so fiercely underground that the foundations of houses and roads were burned away, and, as you know, without foundations no road or building can stand. They collapse! From the outside, the road and the buildings looked as always, but underneath was the raging, unseen fire.

What cannot be seen is just as important as the outside which one can see. The unseen fire did much damage. It is important for the outside of the cup to be clean, but it is even more important that the inside of the cup, which cannot be seen, be clean, also.

Your mother may say to you, " It is time for your bath." You go and scrub your face and nothing else, and come back saying that you are finished. Mother looks behind your ears and finds—can you guess what? You closely resemble the inside of the cup. (Point to cup dirty on inside.) It is just as important to be clean behind the ears, a place which is not visible, as it is to have a clean face which everyone can see. Then it is time to get dressed for Sunday school. You hurry to get ready, and put on your best clothes. Your face is clean, your clothes are nice, and people turn around to look at you and say, " What a nice boy he seems to be," or " What a nice girl she seems to be." But stop and think a minute. Are you nice and clean in your heart also? Or do you resemble the inside of this cup? (Point to the cup dirty on the inside.)

But, you ask, how can I be pure and clean in my heart, which is not visible? Let us see whether Jesus ever said anything about this. In the twenty-third chapter of Matthew Jesus said, " Woe unto you, scribes and Pharisees, hypocrites! for ye are like unto whited sepulchres, which indeed appear beautiful outward, but are within full of dead men's bones, and of all uncleanness." In those days, on a certain feast day, all the sepulchres, or graves, were whitewashed on the outside to make them look white and clean, but inside they were unclean. Again, Jesus said, " Cleanse first that which is within the cup and platter, that the outside of them be clean also." What did Jesus mean? Exactly what these two cups are trying to tell us. The Pharisees did right when people were watching, otherwise they often did things which were wrong. Jesus meant to say that we ought always to do that which is right, not only because others see us, but because we want to do what is the very best at all times. Sometimes we tell a lie or cheat in playing games or say mean things about our friends, and perhaps no one catches us doing this, because we look nice from the outside. But inwardly, as Jesus said, " the cup must be cleaned," which means the heart must be pure.

It often happens that when we start a lie or lose our tempers and say mean things, we do not realize how we are undermining the best things in life, and, like this cup (point to the cup, dirty on the inside), are becoming dirtier on the inside. We must do our best at all times to be like the cup which is clean, both inside and outside.

11

DOING OUR BEST

Object: A candle.

Story: Will you all watch while I light this candle? See how brightly it shines; it does its very best.

Now let us all pretend that we are living three hundred years ago. Let us enter the log cabin of the first settlers in our country. It is night, and a small lighted candle is standing on the table. Of what use is such a tiny light? It guides our footsteps into the loft in which we sleep. It bravely does its best.

A hundred years roll by. We step into a colonial home. Around the table, upon which stands an oil lamp, sits the family, reading and sewing. They seem to strain their eyes. The lamp burns on steadily, doing its best to send its rays in all directions.

Time marches on, and another hundred years have passed. We are walking on the streets of a city. Who is that coming along the walk? It is the lamplighter; he lights the gas light on the corner. This light keeps our feet from stumbling; it is doing its best to guide our footsteps.

The years pass, and now we are near the end of the nineteenth century. We are visiting in the home of our grandparents. It is getting dark; grandfather pushes a button, and, lo and behold, we see our first electric light. It is doing its best to dispel all darkness and gloom.

The middle of the twentieth century approaches. We stand at the window, looking out into the night. Suddenly a searchlight sends a powerful shaft of light into the sky. High above the clouds it penetrates; it has done its best, for it picks out an airplane miles above.

All these lights, whether great or small, have done their best, beginning with the candle, getting brighter with the oil lamp, shining more brilliantly in the gas lamp, steadily increasing in brilliancy in the electric light, and culminating in power and strength in the searchlight. This little candle is shining its best just as much as the powerful searchlight.

So we must strive to do our best, " you in your small corner and I in mine." Jesus was a great light; He was the light of God. His light shone into a dark world, and by His light we today still find our way to God. Over a hundred and fifty years ago a great light guided our forefathers. That light was George Washington, the " Father of his Country." Under his leadership and guidance our country became a free nation. But we cannot all be great lights like George Washington. That is not necessary. Some of us have to be small lights, like this candle, for they are needed too. The great powerful searchlight cannot be used to light our homes. In many places small lights are more useful than large lights.

Years ago, when the Panama Canal was being dug, many workmen were stricken and died of yellow fever. What caused this terrible disease? After much study, it was decided that the mosquito might be the culprit.

But this had to be proved. So one of the men, Jesse
Lazear, allowed a mosquito laden with yellow fever
germs to sting him, with the result that he contracted
yellow fever and died. Through this unselfish act of
Jesse Lazear the cause and cure of yellow fever were
discovered. He was so small a light that perhaps you
have never heard his name, and yet what great good he
did in the world.

So we in our "small corner" must shine our very
best, for the little and the great are all helpers, they
are all needed. God needs many lights, both great
and small.

12

SPREADING HAPPINESS

Object: A can of Dutch Cleanser.

Story: Here stands a can of Dutch Cleanser. Do I
hear someone ask, "Why do you bring Dutch Cleanser
to church? That is to be used only in the kitchen."
You are right, I cannot use it here in the church. But
I have brought it with me to teach us a lesson. Why
do we use Dutch Cleanser? It wages war on blackened pots and pans, spotted sinks and rusty faucets,
and leaves them shining brightly. Why is this cleanser
called "Dutch Cleanser"? Over across the sea there
is a little country called Holland, whose people are
called the Dutch. The Dutch people scrub and scrub
and scrub, even the streets, until they shine. They

have the reputation of keeping their homes bright and shining. Therefore, the Dutch Cleanser Company has the picture of a Dutch girl chasing dirt and germs on the label of the container. Isn't it wonderful to have such a reputation?

How can we be like the Dutch people or like this can of cleanser which brightens pots and pans? We can brighten the lives of others by making them happy.

Let me tell you a story about Jack and Eva, a brother and sister. One bright summer morning mother called, " Jack and Eva, it is eight o'clock, time to get up." Eva came downstairs singing, " I'll set the table for breakfast, mother." Jack came tramping down with a scowl on his face, saying, " I don't see why we have to get up so early." After breakfast mother suggested that Eva wash the dishes and that Jack mow the lawn. Eva quickly jumped up and said, " I'll wash them up in a hurry and dry them too." But Jack grumbled, " This is my vacation, I don't see why I have to work, I want to play ball." Just before lunch mother discovered that she needed bread. Eva willingly went to the store, had a kind word for the proprietor, and stopped to inquire about granny's health, with a happy smile for each one. In the meantime, Jack was pushing the lawnmower, grumbling continually as he went along.

Was Jack or Eva the " cleanser " that spread brightness and sunshine on whomever he or she met or played with? Which one would you like to resemble?

When Jesus was here on earth about two thousand years ago, He left a trail of brightness and happiness wherever He went. The children followed Him, for He drew them with His smiling personality. When the disciples tried to keep the children away from Him for fear they would be a nuisance, Jesus said, " Let the little children come unto me," for He loved to be surrounded by them.

When Jesus said to Zacchæus, " Today, I am coming to visit you," Zacchæus was so happy that he went around inviting all his friends to come to meet this great, happy personality.

Jesus spread brightness and happiness wherever He went. So we too want to be just like Him. We want people to say, " George (or Jane, or whoever it may be) spreads sunshine wherever he (or she) goes." The can of Dutch Cleanser, the Dutch people, the girl Eva, and, most of all, Jesus, want us to imitate their example. Let us all try to be Sunshine Spreaders.

13

THE NEW YEAR

Objects: Two calendars, one of the old year and the other of the New Year.

Story: In my hands I hold two calendars, one of the old year and the other for the coming year. Looking at the calendar of the old year, I remember many things which have happened. Turning to the calendar of the New Year, I am filled with anticipation, wondering what the new year has in store for me.

Shall we try to recall some of the events which occurred in the past year? (Turn to February 12.) Here is the twelfth of February, which we all know is Lincoln's birthday. Remember, we learned that Lincoln was called " Honest Abe." It would be wonderful if people knew us as " Honest George " or " Honest Mary." But, no, that did not become our name, for sometimes we took just one cooky that we were not supposed to have, or we copied an answer from our classmate's arithmetic paper. Alas, we have not lived up to the example of Lincoln.

However (turn to February 12 of the new calendar), in this coming year there also is a February 12. What an inspiration that gives us! We make up our minds that we will try again. This year we determine to succeed in following the example of " Honest Abe."

Let us turn over the pages of the calendar of the old year. The first Monday in September is Labor Day. Labor means work, does it not? We are reminded that Jesus said, " My Father worketh hitherto, and I work." Jesus worked, and we, too, ought also to work. But we think with shame of the tasks we have left uncompleted, both at home and in school.

We turn again to the new calendar. Is there a day in this New Year set aside especially to honor Labor? Indeed, there is a Labor Day on the new calendar. God is saying to us, " You have another chance, I know that you can do better." With renewed hope, we square our shoulders to the tasks before us.

We turn two pages of the old calendar and pause for a moment as our eyes spy Thanksgiving Day. That reminds us of the legend of " The Two Angels." One morning two angels with bags came down from heaven to collect the prayers of men. They decided to divide the work. The angel with the small bag planned to gather the requests and the complaints. The angel with the large bag decided to collect the praise and " thank you " prayers. Both returned to God greatly discouraged. The angel with the small bag had to make three trips, for there were so many requests and complaints. The other angel searched all day among people who seemed to have all their hearts desired. He returned with only one " thank you " prayer in his big bag. Each gave God his bag. Then God comforted them, saying, " One of my loved ones has given me thanks."

Now, we ask ourselves, " Do we send ' thank you ' prayers to God? " We are forced to acknowledge that we have been ungrateful, we have received many good things but forgotten to be thankful. We have failed again.

We turn with expectation to the calendar of the New Year. Excitedly, we find the November page. We will have a Thanksgiving Day again. This turns our dejection to joy; we have another opportunity to be thankful. We remember the legend of " The Two Angels." Did they come to earth only on one day in the year? The legend does not say. We must always be thankful every day, for who knows?—the " thank you " angel may arrive at any time. We must not disappoint him.

Again we cast our eyes on the calendar of the old year. We discover that at least one day in seven is marked in red ink. It is the Sabbath day, Sunday. Our thoughts go back to the Book of Genesis, to the story of creation. God worked six days and rested on the seventh. Then the Fourth Commandment says, " Remember the Sabbath day, to keep it holy." Let us think of what we have done during the past year on these fifty-two red-letter days. Have we kept them holy? Have we used them for the worship of God? Have we attended church and Sunday school? We must shake our heads and admit that often we stayed in bed, sometimes we went on a picnic, other times we went visiting, and also we tried to find other excuses for not worshiping. We have not always obeyed the Fourth Commandment.

We turn again to the New Year's calendar. We feel that we must make amends. How happy we are to see that on the new calendar also there are fifty-two Sundays. We can, we will, we must, obey that law that God has given to us, " Remember the sabbath day, to keep it holy." With new determination, we will do our best to worship God in church and Sunday school every Sunday.

Once more we turn to the calendar of the old year. We are reminded that in a year there are three hundred sixty-five days. Have we always done our best on every one of them? We must admit that we have fallen short of the mark. Many times we have put off until tomorrow what we should have done today. To-morrow has never come, and much has been left undone.

With joy we turn to the calendar of the New Year. Here, too, we have three hundred sixty-five days, each day a new opportunity. If we do not do a good deed today, January first, we will never be able to do it on this day. Anything we do today is done once and for all. We cannot go back and change anything. We can choose how we will use the day, but after the day is over, nothing can change it. Firmly we resolve to live each day in this New Year as best we can. God will help us to do our best if we but ask Him.

14

A CHRISTMAS GIFT

Object: A necktie wrapped as a Christmas gift.

Story: This is the time of the year when we all look forward to Christmas. You see, I have already received a gift. (Hold up Christmas package.) On the tag we read, " With love to Dad from John." I am going to open it and show you what John sent me. It is a lovely necktie. We boys and men can always use a necktie. (Continue looking into the package.) I am wondering whether there is anything else in this package. Frank, will you come here and examine it? (Frank looks through package.) Well, Frank, have you found anything more? (Frank will answer in the negative.) Frank is not able to find anything more. But I know there is something else. I will tell you what it is. It is love.

" But," you say, " we cannot see love." There are many things in this world that we cannot see, but which are here and very real nevertheless. (Drop empty package.) What drew this package downward? Why did it not go up? There we have an invisible force called gravity, which draws everything toward the center of the earth. We cannot see gravity, but we know it is there. We cannot see love, but I know that there is love wrapped in this Christmas gift.

The word " gift " comes from an old Anglo-Saxon word meaning marriage. We know that when two people are married they love one another. At a wedding we see two such people being married. Then they start housekeeping. It takes more than two persons to make a happy marriage. There is more to marriage than just housekeeping. That something more is what you cannot see. It is love. This necktie is a wonderful gift. It is wonderful because it was given in love. Love should be wrapped in every gift we give. It is the main thing in any gift. " The gift without the giver is bare." I could go to the store and buy this tie, but the thing I am happiest about is that John gave it to me. When he gave me this gift, he gave a part of himself, and that part is the love in his heart for me.

Christmas is a time of love. It is the time of the coming of Christ. " God so loved the world, that he gave his only begotten Son." God gave us Jesus. Why? Because He loved us. The very first Christmas gift, Jesus Christ, was given to us with the love of God. We give gifts to one another on Christmas Day because " God so loved the world that he gave his only begotten Son."

This necktie is a fine gift, but it will wear out. However, the love of John which he wrapped into the package will remain. Long after the tie is worn out and discarded, I will still be remembering John's love. Love for others is never lost or wasted. The Apostle Paul wrote, " Now abideth faith, hope, and love, these three, but the greatest of these is love." John's gift of love will go on and on.

On the first Christmas Day, more than 1900 years ago, God gave us Jesus. Why was that so wonderful? Because Jesus is God's Son. Just think of how hard it is for a father and mother to give up their son. Do you think it would be easy for your father and mother to give you up? God gave us His greatest gift when He gave us Jesus. He must love us very, very much to have done that. God gave us His love when He gave us Jesus, just as John gives me his love when he gives me this necktie.

So Christmas is a time of love. We wrap love in our gifts because God sent us His love when He gave Jesus to us. A boy in an orphanage received a basket of fruit on Christmas Day. Other boys received baskets of fruit also, but they ate all theirs on that day. But this boy set the basket of fruit in his window. When asked why he did this, he said, " I want to show my present so people can see that someone cared for me on Christmas Day." That boy thought more of the love that was packed in that basket than of the fruit itself. The meaning of Christmas is that God sent His love in Jesus.

15

IMPORTANT LITTLE THINGS

Object: A penny.

Story: Today we will begin by using a text found in Mark 12: 15. " Bring me a penny." In my hand I hold a penny. It is the smallest coin we have. We will let it preach a sermon to us.

Suppose I needed help in my business. You offer to help me. If I paid you a penny (hold up penny). the first day, double that the second day, double that amount the third day, and so on, until the end of the month, would you take the job for those wages? If I hired you on that basis I would owe you $5,530,117.12 for the last day of the month alone. Not even the richest man in all the world could afford to hire you by paying you one penny the first day and doubling the amount each day thereafter. One penny multiplies itself again and again, and becomes an enormous sum.

A very small thing can multiply so fast and become so big that it overwhelms us. One day Jane saw a penny, like this one, lying on the table. She took it and bought some candy. Several days later she saw two pennies lying on the dresser, which she slipped into her pocket. A week went by, and Jane took four pennies from her mother's purse. Each time it seemed easier to take what did not belong to her, and, finally, she was caught. Others pointed at her and said, " Jane steals, she is a thief." Jane started with taking one penny (hold up penny), just a little thing, but how mighty it became. A little thing started a big bad habit.

Most big things are made up of a lot of little things. A dollar is made up of a hundred pennies like this one. There was once a temple built in China in a rather unusual way. To the first outdoor service each person attending was asked to bring one brick. Many people came and each brought one brick. Some came many times. Slowly the pile of bricks grew, until at last there were enough to build the great temple. A big temple is made up of bricks, little things.

We often think we should not bother with little things. But it is the little things in life that make us what we are. We can build up a noble life with little daily actions. Sometimes we can help another boy or girl at school, sometimes run errands for mother, or flash a little smile that will brighten the day for someone. All these little things added together will do more good than one big heroic act. The little things do count.

One Sunday morning some years ago a little girl six

years of age came to a small Sunday school. The classes were so full and the church so small that there was no room for her. Disappointed, she returned home. However, without telling anyone, she decided to save her pennies, like this one, so that the church might be built larger. She became very ill and died. Under her pillow was found a little red purse containing fifty-seven pennies and a little scrap of paper, on which was written, " These pennies are to build a larger church." The story of the little pocketbook and the fifty-seven pennies got into the newspapers. When people read the story, they began to send money to the minister of this little church, and soon the fifty-seven pennies grew into $250,000. The church that was built is the Baptist Temple on Broad Street in Philadelphia. Temple University is connected with this church, and in one of its halls hangs a picture of Hattie May Wiatt, the little girl who saved fifty-seven pennies. Only a penny (show penny), not worth much, but see what Hattie's pennies did.

There are over three hundred boys and girls enrolled in our Sunday school. Suppose each one saved an extra penny like this one every week. That would mean three dollars every Sunday, or one hundred fifty-six dollars in a year. One hundred fifty-six dollars to help the poor, to send to the missions, or to beautify our church building. What a big sum can grow from one little insignificant penny!

We have proved that little things do count. One little wrong thing done every day soon forms one bad habit. Little kindnesses performed daily make one noble life. One penny saved systematically helps those in need. Make the little things count, they are important.

16

THE SIGNIFICANCE OF THE PULPIT

Object: The pulpit.

Story: Today I will give you a biography. A biography is a story of someone's life. This is a biography of the pulpit. So listen to the story of the pulpit. It is one of the important objects in God's house, the church. It has been used for many, many years. The first time it is mentioned in the Bible is in the Book of Nehemiah. This happened at least three thousand years ago. Ezra, the scribe, read the book of The Law of Moses to the Israelites from a pulpit. Ever since that long-ago time pulpits have been used in the churches.

It is usually made of wood in a design which harmonizes with the architecture of the church in which it stands. The design of ours is Gothic. The carved arch on the sides has a point at the center which reminds us of hands with finger tips placed together in prayer. It is a constant reminder that the church is the House of Prayer.

In some churches the pulpit is placed up very high, to remind us that Christ often preached from a mountain top. Usually it is set on a specially built platform in the front of the congregation, so that the people may see and hear the man who speaks to them.

But the pulpit is not only a piece of furniture, it is also a symbol. There is a reason for its presence in the House of God.

Who is the man who stands behind it? What is his business here in the church? We call him a preacher, a minister, or a pastor. He is not an orator or a politi-

cian. He stands before you to tell you about God, our
heavenly Father, and about His Son Jesus. He tells
you how willing and anxious God is to help you, not
only when you are in trouble but at all times. He tries
to teach you how to live a good life. In the words of
the Great Commandment he says, " Thou shalt love
the Lord, thy God; and thy neighbor as thyself."

I suppose you are asking yourself the question,
" How does the preacher know all those things? "   I
will try to tell you. Look on the top of the pulpit.
There you will see a Book—the greatest Book in the
world, the best seller of all times—the Bible. At school
you read and study your history to learn about the people who lived before you. The doctor has gone to
school to learn how to care for sick people. The
preacher also has gone to school, has read and studied
the Bible to learn the truths contained in it. After
much hard work and preparation, he stands before
you to help you understand the Word of God.

Then you hear the preacher say, " Let us bow our
heads." A feeling of quietness spreads from the pulpit
throughout the congregation. God seems very near to
us as, together with the minister, we bow our heads in
prayer. God listens and hears the prayers offered from
the pulpit. As the preacher's " amen " is said, all raise
their heads. They realize that in prayer they have
been brought into the presence of God.

From all this we see that the pulpit is not only a
beautifully carved piece of wood, but that it has a
greater significance. It carries and supports the Bible,
which is God's Word to us. It is not like a table on
which are laid all kinds of books and magazines. It
has the honor of carrying the greatest Book in all the
world, the Bible. From it the minister explains the

Bible and tells the people what God wants them to do. And facing the pulpit, we bow our heads, and over it the minister bows his head, and together we pray to our heavenly Father.

17

THE LAST SUPPER

Object: The Lord's Table.

Story: Here before us stands a table. Can a table teach us anything? That depends on the kind of table it is. This is the Lord's Table. It differs from other tables, for on one side of it are written these words, " In Remembrance of Me." What do these words, " in remembrance," mean? They mean, to call back to our memory.

Many years ago there lived in Scotland a poor widow. Her home was very poor, but on the shelf of her cupboard stood an old cracked cup covered with a glass bowl. This cup was of great value to the widow, for it reminded her that Queen Victoria had stopped in front of her home because she was thirsty. The widow brought her a cold drink in that old cracked cup. Therefore the cup was set on the shelf with a glass bowl to cover it. Every time anyone noticed it standing there, the widow would say, " I have kept it for many years in remembrance of Queen Victoria." Notice the words, " in remembrance."

In the Bible we read of Zacchæus, a little short man who climbed a tree so that he could see Jesus passing by. Jesus saw him, spoke to him, visited him, and

Zacchæus became one of His followers. There is a legend told about this Zacchæus. Early every morning he took a walk and came home happy and cheerful. His wife finally became so curious that one day she decided to follow him. Where do you suppose she found him? She found him under the tree which he had climbed the first time he had seen Jesus. Here he remembered and recalled everything that Jesus had done for him.

Let us now return to the Lord's Table and the words, "In Remembrance of Me." The widow had a cup in remembrance of Queen Victoria. Zacchæus remembered Jesus best when he was under the tree where he had first seen Him. On the Lord's Table we read "In Remembrance of Me." This "Me" means Jesus Christ. Why ought we to remember Jesus?

On the last night of Jesus' life here on earth He and His twelve disciples ate supper together. This was Jesus' last supper. I think that you have all seen the painting *The Last Supper*, by Leonardo da Vinci, depicting Jesus and His disciples sitting around a table. At this time Jesus told His disciples what He wished them to do in order to remember Him. Do you think He asked them to erect a monument or build a temple in His honor? No, Jesus took a loaf of bread and divided it among them. He also passed around a cup of wine, and said, "Do this in remembrance of me." He set up a simple meal as a memorial to Himself. When, occasionally, you see a white cloth on this Lord's Table and see the plates with bread and the cups with wine, you know that it is "Communion Sunday." You know that we expect to celebrate the Lord's Supper around His table in remembrance of Him.

Whenever we read the words on the Lord's Table,

"In Remembrance of Me," we are reminded that God sent His only Son to earth, that He died for us, that He rose again from the dead, and that He is with us always. He said, "Lo, I am with you alway, even unto the end of the world."

18

MUSIC IN WORSHIP

Object: The pipe organ.

Story: Our text today is found in Psalm 150: 4: "Praise him with stringed instruments and organ." David tells us in this psalm that an organ is a very helpful object with which to praise God. The organ is a very ancient instrument. In Genesis 4: 21 we read, "Jubal was the father of all such as handle the harp and the organ." Jubal was the grandson of Adam, who was the father of all mankind. Of course, this organ that Jubal made was not like our organ today. It was made from the horns of cattle, from five to twenty-three in number. The music of the first organs was produced by people blowing on those horns. From this crude beginning developed the pipe organ, an instrument like the one we have before us.

"But," you ask, "why do we need a pipe organ or music here in the church?" God put plenty of music in the world—the song of birds, the babbling of brooks, the whispering of the winds, and the melody of the human voice. Since there is so much music in nature which God has made, why do we need music in the church? In the one hundred fiftieth Psalm we are told to praise God in the church with musical instruments. The Bible asks us to use music in our worship service in the church.

What kind of music shall we use? When Napoleon was crossing the Alps, only a few of his soldiers were marching onward firmly and steadily. The majority were tired, worn out, and lagging behind. Napoleon ordered the band to play a stirring march. The soldiers cheered, they caught the marching step, and moved forward in a solid column. The music turned their tiredness into new strength and their discouragement into new hope. The prelude, the first music played on the organ at our service, ought to be music that brings us into the right attitude for worship. Just as the band gave renewed hope to the soldiers, so the organ lifts our hearts in praise to God.

Singing has always been a part of religion. The Hebrews had a singing religion. They had the Book of Psalms, the mother hymn book of all the world. Jesus and His disciples sang. The early Christians sang; even when going to their death they had a song of praise on their lips. Christians have continued singing through the centuries. Today the singing of hymns is a vital part of our worship service. And the organ is important because it leads us as we sing these hymns of praise to God.

Then we hear the organ playing the offertory. It tells us that now is the time to bring an offering, our gifts, to God. It reminds us that God so loved the world that He gave His only Son, the best gift ever given in this world. If God gave His best, can we do less?

At the end of the service the church is filled with the music of the postlude. The sermon, the prayers, and the music have brought us into the presence of God. While we are leaving the House of God, the organ tries to impress upon us the sacredness of the hour we have spent together.

So we find that music has a great place in our lives. Music is a universal language. We may not be able to understand the languages of other peoples, but we can all understand music. It unites our hearts. The organ is the most perfect musical instrument, for in it are combined the trumpet, the violin, the flute, the harp, and many others. It is the instrument on which all these other instruments can be played by one person. The organ is a very helpful instrument in our church.

19

THE LOVE OF JESUS
(Good Friday)

Object: A cross.

Story: To Christian people everywhere the Cross of Jesus Christ is the most holy and sacred thing in the world. Why is this so?

The symbol of the cross is a common one. We see it on church steeples and in our churches, and we wear it on watch chains and necklaces. We read about it in the Bible and sing of it in our hymns. Truly, it is the most loved symbol in all the world.

This was not always true. Before the time of Jesus it was an instrument of torture, a despised object used in the execution of criminals. It was a repulsive thing hated by all good people.

Over nineteen hundred years ago there lived in Palestine the best Person who ever walked on this earth, Jesus Christ. He was unjustly condemned to die on the cross. The best Person in the world was to be put on a cross where before only criminals had hung. This changed the cross from a despised object used only for wicked men to a loved one, because Jesus, an innocent person, suffered and died on it. His enemies mocked Him, saying, " He saved others, himself he cannot save."

How was it that Jesus could save others but Himself He could not save? Let me explain in a story why this was so. I think that the story of John Maynard will help you to understand. John Maynard was the pilot of a ship on Lake Erie. One summer day he had a crowd of people on board. Suddenly, he saw black smoke coming from below. After investigation it was discovered that the ship was on fire. Water was thrown on the flames, but it was impossible to save the ship. The ship was seven miles from land. The fire was in the front of the ship. The captain ordered the passengers and crew to the other end, where there was the least danger. John Maynard remained at his post. Smoke and flames billowed about him. The heat became more intense; he could not see the shore. The captain called through a megaphone, " Hold on five minutes more." John Maynard guided his ship to the shore, saved all on board but lost his own life. John Maynard could have saved himself, but he did not want to. Jesus could have saved Himself, but His great heart of love would not let Him. He died for us on the cross and believing that He did this for us, we are saved.

The symbol of the cross reminds us of the self-sacrifice of Jesus. Every time we see it we are reminded of the love of Jesus.

Norman McLeod told a story of a widow in Scotland. She was unable to pay her rent, so the landlord threatened to put her out. She decided to take her only child, a boy ten years of age, and walk across the hills to the home of a relative. The day was bright and sunshiny, but toward evening it became bitterly cold, and a terrible snowstorm started. When they failed to arrive, a party of men was sent out to search for them. They found the mother with very few clothes on, dead in the snow. Searching further, they found the son in a sheltered place, safe, wrapped in his mother's clothes. She loved her only child so much that she gave her life to save him.

So the cross on which Jesus was crucified is not only a symbol of sacrifice but also of love. Jesus loved us so much, just as the Scotch mother loved and died for her son, that He died for us on the cross. Therefore, when we see the cross we are reminded of Jesus, our Savior. He changed the cross from a despised object to something that reminds us of His love and sacrifice.

20

A CALL TO WORSHIP

Object: A bell.

Story: Most church buildings have a tower, steeple or spire, in which hangs a bell very much like this one which I hold in my hand, only much larger. Throughout the world the church bells ring, calling one and all to worship. In the Bible, in the twenty-eighth chapter of Exodus, we read about the first time the bell was used to call people to worship. Aaron, the high priest, wore a robe on which were sewed small golden bells, which tinkled as he walked. This was to indicate that it was time for worship service.

It will be of interest for you to know that the oldest dated Christian bell hangs in the tower of St. Stephen's Episcopal Church in East Haddam, Connecticut. It was bought from a cargo of old metal which arrived from Spain in the year 1840. On it there is an inscription written in Spanish and Latin: " Corrales has made me in the year of our Lord, 815."

So down through the centuries has come the music of church bells. They ring out across the hills and valleys from country churches, peal forth their sound to the crowds from city churches, and chime from towering cathedrals. As we hear the music of the church bell we look up to the church tower and feel that here is a language which we can all understand.

The church bell calls us to friendliness. There are times when we feel lonely. Then we hear the ringing of the church bell. It seems to say, " Come to church to meet your friends. Here you will find others who feel and think as you do." So we answer the call of the bell. We go into the church. We sit together, and it seems as if a feeling of friendliness passes from one to the other, and at the same time we all feel closer to God. We return to our homes feeling happy that we listened to the call of the church bell.

The deep tone of the bell calls us to loyalty. It always rings exactly at the same time on Sundays. It does not ring at one hour one Sunday and at another hour the next Sunday. This means that the church bell is dependable and faithful. The bell rings regularly and not only once in a while. So we ought always to be loyal and dependable like the church bell. Every time we hear the bell it should remind us of God. The faithfulness and dependability of the church bell should be a constant reminder to us that we be faithful and loyal to God. We can show our loyalty by regular attendance at the worship services in our church.

The church bell calls us to happiness. What joyful tones it sends forth at Christmas, New Year's, and Easter! At Christmas we hear the song of the angels, " Unto you is born this day . . . a Savior, which is Christ the Lord. Glory to God in the highest and on earth peace, good will to men." At New Year's it peals forth, " The Old Year is past, a new one is beginning, look forward to the future with great hope." And at Easter in stately tones it announces " Christ the Lord is risen today." What messages of joy it brings to our hearts and minds!

Sunday after Sunday the bell calls us to worship. " Come and worship, come and worship Christ the Lord! " I think most of you are familiar with Millet's beautiful painting *The Angelus*. It is a picture of the close of day. A man and his wife who are working in a field bow their heads in worship at the sound of the bell from the church in the distance. The real purpose of the church bell is to call us to worship. In our busy lives we must pause to worship God. Our church bell, too, calls us to worship. We answer its call. We enter God's house and bow our heads in prayer. In the midst of our busy life this quiet hour spent in communion with God gives us strength and hope to go on. We are thankful for the bell because it calls us to friendliness, loyalty, happiness and worship.

21

SHOES FOR ROUGH ROADS

Objects: A pair of worn walking shoes.

Story: Our text this morning is found in the Book of Deuteronomy, chapter thirty-three, verses twenty-five and twenty-seven: " Thy shoes shall be iron and brass." " The eternal God is thy refuge, and underneath are the everlasting arms."

These words, " Thy shoes shall be iron and brass," were spoken by Moses thousands of years ago to the tribe of Asher. He had been giving advice to all the tribes under his leadership, and to the tribe of Asher he said, " Thy shoes shall be iron and brass." This seems like strange advice, does it not? The tribe of Asher lived in the rough and hilly section of the country. The hills were steep and the rocks over which people had to walk were sharp and pointed. So Moses told them that they needed a pair of good strong shoes (hold up walking shoes) to stand the wear and the tear of this rough country.

As the tribe of Asher needed shoes of iron and brass to journey over their rough and rugged hills, so we need good strong shoes to follow the path that Christ has pointed out to us. Christ said that it would not be easy to follow Him.

This pair of shoes looks worn and scuffed, as if they had seen hard usage. They have tramped over miles and miles of rough roads. They show us that they have encountered rocks and stones along the way. So it is in life.

In the year 1875 there came to this country from

Alsace Lorraine a family with seven children, named Kindleberger. When Jacob, one of the children, was ten years of age, he was sent to work in the paper mills, where he earned twenty-five cents a day. In five years he was earning only thirty cents a day. He could neither read nor write and had no ambition.

But one Sunday evening something happened which entirely changed his life. He went to church for the purpose of laughing at the service. But as he listened to the minister preach, he became dissatisfied with his life. He determined to learn to read and write. It was uphill work for him, for his eyesight was very poor. When he was twenty-one years of age, he entered the fourth grade. He earned his living as janitor of the school. In four years' time, however, he entered the university to study for the ministry. He set his face toward this goal. But it was not to be, his eyes became more troublesome, and he either had to leave college or go blind. What a disappointment! What a hard knock!

What was he to do? Finally, he became a very successful salesman. Later, he decided to open a new paper mill near Kalamazoo, Michigan, where now stands the town of Parchment. Success came slowly. But now the mills are among the largest in the world. "Uncle Jake," as he is affectionately known, started a Sunday school, and now there is a fine church in the town. He has been the teacher of the Adult Bible Class for many years. The uneducated immigrant boy, treading the difficult way of life, steadfastly set his face toward the goal, and has become "Uncle Jake," well-beloved and successful business man.

From this story we learn that "Uncle Jake's" life was not easy; it was a hard, rough road that he had to travel. These shoes remind us that the road is rough and difficult. If we want to reach our goal and do something worth while we will not find it easy.

Moses not only told the tribe of Asher that they needed shoes of iron and brass, but in the second verse of the text he says, " The eternal God is thy refuge and underneath are the everlasting arms." Moses said that God would always be there helping and watching over us. God watching over us is very much like the captain of a big ship watching over the passengers. The sea may be very rough, but the passengers depend upon the captain to get them safely to the harbor. They trust him; they believe that he knows how to guide the ship. The captain watches over all his passengers through fog, rain, and storm.

In the same way God watches over us when our path in life seems hard and we become discouraged. These shoes (hold them up) show that they have gone along a hard and rough road. But they protected the feet of the person who wore them. God protects us. When we have God with us it is much easier to travel a rough road. In fact, this is the best and only way to travel any road.

22

THE PRINTS THAT WE LEAVE

Object: A finger print.

Story: The dictionary defines a finger print as a method of personal identification widely employed at the present time. Let us look at this card on which we see a finger print. This is a print of my thumb. Suppose we should all stand around a highly polished table and each of us press our thumbs on its surface. Then we would call in a finger print expert, a man who can identify prints. Do you think he would be able to match my print with any of those on the table? Or might there be several of us who would have exactly the same print? It has been estimated that not once in ten thousand years would the finger prints of two people be the same. Therefore, the expert could easily match my print on the table with the one on this card. We can always be identified by our finger prints.

Every criminal is finger-printed by our police departments. If he should escape from prison, no matter how he disguises himself, he can always be identified by his finger prints.

Shall we try to do some identifying by studying some finger prints which have been left for us to read? These finger prints will not be like the one on this card, which only an expert can read. But the prints and impressions of which I am thinking, all of us can read. They are found all around us.

As we walk in the great out-of-doors we see the wonder in nature. We behold the blue sky and the fleecy clouds above us, the high hills and mountains in the distance, and the river flowing peacefully in the valley. We marvel at the giant oak, the greenness of the fir tree, the beautiful color of the rose and the flash of the wings of the bird flying by. Whose finger prints do we see in all these wonders? You are right. They are God's. No one but He could make everything so perfectly.

Are God's the only finger prints we are able to read? Let us read the finger prints of people who lived hundreds and thousands of years ago.

In my ears I hear a bold demand, " Let my people go." Moses spoke these words. His people, the Israelites, were slaves in Egypt. He led them to freedom into the new land of Canaan. Moses also gave the Ten Commandments to the world. The finger print on this card is mine; it identifies me. Every time we read the Ten Commandments we see the prints of Moses, they identify him.

Many years after Moses lived, Jesus came to earth. Jesus was God's Son, who lived on the earth only thirty-three years. He died on a cross for us. Wherever we see a cross we see the prints of Jesus. The cross identifies Him. He founded the Christian Church. We see His prints in the Church. His prints also are engraved on the hearts of all His followers. Yes, there are many prints of Himself that Jesus left for us to read.

A little man named Paul became a follower of Jesus. He made long journeys telling about Christ. One day in a vision he heard a call, " Come over to Macedonia (Europe) to help us." He obeyed this call, which made him the first missionary. His prints are found in every missionary up to the present day.

The years pass. Martin Luther leaves his indelible prints on the hearts of all Protestants. In the lives of the nurses in our hospitals we see the prints of the unselfish life of Florence Nightingale. In our churches we hear the immortal music of a Handel, whose greatest composition, " The Messiah," stirs our hearts. We gaze with awe at the beautiful paintings of the artist da Vinci. We receive bodily comfort from the great inventions of a man like Thomas Edison. All these, and many others, have left their finger prints for us to read.

Let us do something worth while in this world, so that those who come after us can see and read our prints. The finger print on this card is mine; it identifies me. Why not try to do something so good and so worth while that people will remember you by it. We should leave our prints behind us in the good deeds that we do.

23

THE GREATEST ROCK

Object: A rock.

Story: Forty miles above the city of Wanhsien in China there stands a high rock that draws the attention of all who pass by. It is called " The Precious Rock." The Chinese tell the following story about the rock. Many years ago a poor Buddhist priest was walking along the road. As he came near this rock he decided to rest, for he was tired and hungry. All at once, looking upward, he saw rice pouring out of a hole in the rock, and heard a voice saying, " Take what you need." The supply stopped as soon as he had taken enough for one day. He stayed there for a number of days and daily received his portion of rice. Then he left and spread the news, and although the miracle stopped, the rock became a sacred place. A temple was built on the rock and pilgrims came from all parts of the country to worship. This was a precious rock for the priest, but only for him, for when his needs were satisfied, the miracle ceased.

I would like to tell you of another rock, the most

wonderful rock of all. In 1 Corinthians 10: 4 we read,
" And that rock was Christ." Here Christ is called
a rock. Let me tell you about Him. The Buddhist
priest received rest and food from " The Precious
Rock." What blessings come to us from *Christ* the
rock?

(Hold up rock.) What good can we get from a rock
like this one? If you think this rock is too small to
be of any use, just close your eyes and imagine that
it is a tremendous rock.

Now let us think back to the traveler of ancient days
who walked along poor roads and in the hot summer
days felt the need of relief from the blistering sun and
the hot winds. Therefore, when he came upon a great
rock standing on a treeless plain, he gratefully sat
down in its shade. That is the thought Isaiah had
when he wrote, " The shadow of a great rock in a weary
land." That is what Jesus Christ is. He said, " Come
unto me, and I will give you rest." He offers us cool
shade, rest from whatever troubles us. Whatever
bothers you in your home, at school, or at play, go tell
it to Christ. You will find that He cares for us.

Again, we look at this rock and through our magni-
fying glasses it looks immense. What else can Christ
the rock do for us? A large rock can be a refuge.
Have any of you ever made the trip through the Cave
of the Winds at Niagara Falls? As you walk along
you get soaking wet with spray from the tumbling
water. The water from the high falls is in your eyes
and the roaring in your ears. Finally, you find your
way across a wooden bridge. All at once you have
found relief from the pounding of the water. You
look around and see that you are walking between two
immense masses of rock. They shelter you from the

spraying waters. On these rocks is a sign which reads, " The Rock of Ages." It is a refuge from the hard, beating water. So Christ is our refuge. With our hand in His we can ward off temptation. He protects us. He is a refuge from danger. He will guard us from all harm and evil.

Once more we cast our eyes on this rock and in imagination it assumes huge proportions. We now see it as the solid rock foundation of a large church. In Johnstown, New York, there stands such a church. When the flood carried away all the buildings in the vicinity, the church, although the flood flowed through the entire building, stood firmly because it had a solid rock foundation.

Christ is like such a rock foundation on which we can build. The floods cannot wash away this foundation, because Christ is greater than any flood. One time, when Jesus and His disciples were on the sea, a storm threatened to upset their boat. But Jesus was greater than the storm. He calmed the sea. We do not have to be afraid when we are with Christ. We can safely build our lives on Him. He is like a rock foundation.

A sailor was shipwrecked at sea. The waves washed him on a high rock. He clung to it until he was finally saved. When he was asked if he trembled while clinging to the rock, he said, " Yes, I trembled, but the rock didn't." Christ is like a rock. We may be afraid, but He is not; we may tremble, but He does not.

We sing, " On Christ the solid rock I stand." What I hold in my hand is a rock, but Christ is the best rock of all. He offers us rest, refuge, and a firm foundation on which to build our lives.

24

" CONSIDER THE LILIES "
(Children's Day)

Object: A lily or any other flower.

Story: Today is Children's Day. Because we are surrounded by so many beautiful flowers I have chosen as my text the words of Jesus, " Consider the lilies of the field." Jesus, the greatest preacher who ever lived, was preaching His first sermon. He was on a hillside with the people about Him when He looked down into the valley where the beautiful lilies were blooming, and calling their attention to them, He said, " Consider the lilies of the field." What a scene that must have been! What a simple text, yet how wonderful! God made those lilies. He painted their colors with sunlight, watered them with dew and showers, and dressed them in colors grander than " Solomon in all his glory " wore.

In my hands I hold a lily. As I look at it and examine it closely, I am reminded of the words of the poet, when he looked at a flower growing in a crevice in the wall, " If I knew what you are, root and all and all in all, I would know what God and man is."

As we look at this beautiful flower, we, too, are filled with wonder—wonder at its breath-taking beauty. Some of us never seem to notice the beautiful. " Give us something useful," we say, " and never mind about its being beautiful." But God wants us to love beauty. There is scarcely anything which gives us more wonderful thoughts of God than to look at this flower. See the pains God has taken to make it beautiful.

When Jesus said, " Consider the lilies of the field,"

He surely meant that we should live beautiful lives. God's plan for us is something altogether lovely. If we are worried and disappointed we may be sure that we are not living the beautiful life which God meant us to live. Something has gone wrong; in some way we think that we know better than God. He has meant us to grow a certain way, to become beautiful in His sight, and we have been trying something else. So we must go right to Him and ask Him to make us lovely too.

This lily is not only beautiful, it is also fragrant. It is pouring forth its perfume, spending itself to do others good. And so it tells us what God is. He is not a statue whose beauty we admire, He is alive and good. Jesus said that God shows His goodness in love for us and therefore He is our Father.

As we see the beauty and breathe the fragrance of this lily, it makes us believe in a God. For who but God could make so beautiful a flower? When Napoleon was Emperor of France he put a man named Charney into prison, because he thought he was an enemy of the government. Charney's prison opened into a small yard surrounded by an iron fence. He did not believe in God, and wrote on the prison wall these words, " All things come by chance."

One day, while walking back and forth in his prison yard, he spied a tiny green plant breaking through the ground. This pleased him very much, for there was not another green thing to be seen. He watched it grow every day. In his loneliness the plant became his friend. When the plant started to grow a bud and the bud started to open, he was happy. The flower was white and rose-colored, with a fine silvery fringe. Charney watered it with the water brought to him by the jailer for his own thirst.

As he watched the little flower it seemed to whisper to him, " There is One who has made me so wonderfully beautiful and that One is God." This thought convinced Charney that he was wrong when he wrote on the wall, " All things come by chance." So he erased those words and substituted, " He who made all things is God."

The wife of the jailer had been watching Charney care for the flower. She told the story of his love for the plant to a friend of hers, and finally it came to the ears of the Empress Josephine. The Empress said, " The man who so loves and tends a flower cannot be a bad man," and she persuaded the Emperor to free him. So Charney was set at liberty and carried his flower home with him. It had taught him to believe in God and had freed him from prison.

Look at this flower, see its beauty and drink in its fragrance. It, too, convinces us that there must be One guiding hand, one God, over us all, who has made us and the entire universe.

25

THE INEXTINGUISHABLE LIGHT

Object: A candle.

Story: I think every one of us remembers the story of how, back in Old Testament times, God called the young boy Samuel. In this story we read, " The lamp of God was not yet gone out." What can those words, " lamp of God," mean? Hundreds of years before the time of Samuel, rules had been made not only on how to worship in God's temple but also on the proper use of its furnishings. One of these rules stated that the "lamp of God" should be alight "from evening until morning." While darkness prevailed there was to be one source of light, the lamp of God. The Israelites brought to the temple olive oil, which was used to fill this lamp. The oil to keep the lamp burning was brought by the people. This lamp of God shed its light on the Holy Place in the temple. No darkness could put out that light.

No darkness can ever extinguish the light of this candle which I have here. All the blackness in the world can make no impression on the flame. Indeed, the blacker and darker it is, the more light the candle seems to throw in every direction.

During a London blackout a father and son were stumbling along in the inky darkness. The father was getting angrier and angrier about the hardships caused by the war. The son was paying no attention to the grumbling of his father, for he was looking into the sky. Suddenly he said, "Dad, look, when it's so dark you can see the stars better." How this cheered the father! Even if the lights had gone out all over Europe, the stars still shone. Because it was so dark they seemed brighter than ever before. And behind the stars was God, "keeping watch above His own." The stars shining in darkness remind us that the "lamp of God has not yet gone out," and that such stars bring us hope and cheer. All the darkness in the world cannot dim the stars, any more than it can black out this candle light. If the darkness were as black as pitch in this room, it still would not be able to put out this light.

Two thousand years ago Jesus came to this earth.

Can you hear Him saying, "I am the light of the world"? Then turning to His twelve disciples, He said, "Ye are the light of the world." And then comes the most important verse, "Let your light shine." Jesus was crucified. Was God's lamp out? Was there only darkness? If all the electric lights in the church building were out, could the darkness put out this candle? No, never. So, also, Jesus sent out a group of men to preach and teach for Him. They were to be light-bearers.

Then came Paul, our first foreign missionary, who carried the light of God from Asia to Europe. Paul was beheaded. Was the light out? Was the darkness too great for the light? Indeed not! We see the light of God springing up in the lives of the early Christians, who courageously kept the flame burning, though often their bodies became living torches. These early Christians were tortured, imprisoned, thrown to the lions and killed, but all this could not put out the light of God that was in them. Through their persistent light-bearing amidst the great darkness of heathenism Christianity became the religion of the Roman world. No darkness, even though the years in which they lived were called the Dark Ages, could overwhelm the divine flame they carried.

Suppose we carried this candle into a dark cellar in which there was no window or any electric lights, could the darkness extinguish the flame? No, it would still burn on bravely.

On we go to the Middle Ages, when John Hus in Bohemia holds high the torch of Christ. John Hus was burned at the stake, but the glowing embers of that bonfire were scattered into every European country. From there they came across the ocean to America, creating a land of freedom to worship as we pleased. The light-bearers are still carrying the " lamp of God " to every land and nation. No darkness has ever been able to extinguish that lamp.

If we should take this candle into the darkest hole imaginable, even that darkness could make no impression on this flame. It would still be burning brightly. The fact is, it does not go out, it cannot go out.

This candle finally will burn itself out. But the " lamp of God " never goes out. It is always shining in some one of us. God wants every one of us to be bearers of His light. Whenever we stand up against wrong, live up to our ideals, help someone in need, or tell others about Jesus, we are keeping " the lamp of God " shining.

26

CAUGHT IN A TRAP

Object: A mousetrap.

Story: One night Mr. and Mrs. Mouse called their family together for a conference. At the meeting there were present Papa and Mamma Mouse, Big Brother Mouse, Middle-sized Mouse, and Squeaky Mouse. A new object had come to rest before the entrance to their home which we call a mousetrap. (Hold up mousetrap.)

The Mouse family were sitting around the trap talking. Papa Mouse pointed to it and said, " Do you know what it is? "

The baby mouse, whose name was Squeaky, was the

first to answer. "I see a piece of cheese on it and I want to eat it because I am hungry," he said.

"Don't be foolish, Squeaky," said Papa Mouse. "That thing is a trap, and the cheese was put on it by someone to tempt some stupid mouse like you. Surely the cheese is good, but if you should try to get it, the trap will spring and kill you."

Then Middle-sized Mouse said, "Perhaps that is the reason our neighbor mice all walked right by the trap. Not any of them tried to get the cheese. A trap! Well, that is something of which to be afraid."

"Yes," said Mamma Mouse, "you will notice that the one who set the trap put cheese on it, the very food we mice like the best. The idea of trying to tempt us with cheese."

"I don't think the trap is as dangerous as all that," finally said Big Brother Mouse. "Everyone is afraid of it. We know the cheese has been put there to tempt us, but I am not afraid of temptation. It is fun to flirt with temptation. You and all the neighbors are afraid, but I am not. Here is my chance to become famous and a real hero. I'll get the cheese and when the other mice of the village see how brave and strong I am, they will make me their king."

From the shadows there stepped an old, grey, limping, short-tailed mouse. It was Grandpa Mouse. He said, "Listen to me, Big Brother. I talk from experience. Look at me. I limp as you all know and I have only half a tail. I surely am a pathetic looking mouse. I once talked like Big Brother. The cheese is a terrible temptation. My advice is to stay away from temptation as far as possible. The one who put the cheese there is not anxious for you to have good food. With it he wants to lead you to your death. See what hap-

pened to me. The trap snapped; I was caught by paw
and tail. I succeeded in freeing myself with the help
of others, but I must always bear these marks. Follow my advice and keep away from the cheese."

Big Brother Mouse only laughed and called Grandpa
an old fossil and said, " You think because you were
caught, everyone else will be. I am wiser than you
are."

So they separated. That night Big Brother Mouse
yielded to the tempting cheese. We all know what
happened. He was killed. If he had only stayed far
away from temptation.

Life is full of traps. These traps have bait on them
just as this mousetrap has cheese. A boy in school
wants high grades to be at the top of his class. It is
good to have high grades, but if you are tempted to
get high grades by cheating, then it is a trap. Sometimes we are tempted to cheat. It is a trap; do not go
near it. A girl keeps company with bad companions.
Watch out; it is a trap. The bait on this trap is all
kinds of fun and pleasure. But fun and pleasure with
evil companions is a trap. Stay away from it. A
young man wants to get rich fast. He is tempted to be
dishonest, to take money that does not belong to him.
It is a trap; he will only be caught.

When we are tempted, let us do what Jesus did. He
looked to God, His Father, for help, and then temptation lost its power over Him.

27

CHRIST IS THE DOOR

Object: A door.

Story: One day Jesus was sitting on the Mount of Olives with His disciples. Directly below them they could see the wall about the city of Jerusalem. In this wall, at various intervals, were gates through which to enter the city. Just below Jesus and His disciples could be seen one of these gates, called the Sheep Gate. It was through this gate that the sheep which were destined for sacrifice in the temple entered the city. Jesus saw a flock of sheep coming up the valley and pass into the city through this narrow gate. And so, according to His usual way of speaking of that which was passing before His eyes, He turned to His disciples and said, " I am the door."

When we look at a door (point to one of the church doors) we wonder what Jesus meant when He said, " I am the door."

The ancient Romans did not believe in just one God as we do, but in many gods. One of these gods was called Janus, and his name means the " god of the door." So they called the first month of the year January, because it is at the door of the year. The door is what you must go through before you get inside any place. January is the month by which we enter the New Year. February does not let us into the New Year. January, coming first among the months, is the door of the year.

As the month of January is the door into the New Year, so Jesus is the door into the Kingdom of Heaven.

Jesus often spoke of the Kingdom of Heaven. By that He meant not only a heaven in the next world, but a heaven into which we can go right now. Heaven is where God is. If we have God in our hearts now we are in heaven. We can have God in our hearts now, and then we have heaven in us. Therefore, Jesus is the door to heaven.

The right way to get into this church is by way of that door. (Point to it.) To attempt entrance by any other way is to arouse suspicion. That door opens for anyone who really wants to get into this church. Jesus is the door which opens for anyone who wants to enter the Kingdom of Heaven. He has no favorites. Everyone, young and old, rich and poor, white, yellow, brown, or black may enter. There is no use trying to climb over the wall or crawling through the windows. You would not enter this church in that way. You use the door. Christ is the door into the Kingdom of Heaven. He must admit you.

Into what does this church door admit you? Of course, it lets you into the church. But that is not all. The real reason why that door opens is to let you into the presence of God. When that door swings wide to let you in, it is a hearty welcome by God. Jesus is the door to God, and He gives us a warm welcome.

But this door not only gives us entrance into the church, it also is to be used for an exit. We must also go out of this door into the world and to our work again. This door not only says, " Come in," but also, " Go! " In that way, too, Jesus is like a door. He says, " Come," and then He says, " Go! " After we have " come " to Jesus, then we must " go " to tell others about Him. It is not enough for us to come; we must go to others and tell them to come. We must tell them that Jesus is like a door, through which we must go to come to God.

Sir Wilfred Grenfell was a great doctor in England. As a young man he always came into the church through a door very much like this one. There he heard about Jesus, who became for him the door that led him into the presence of God. The door welcomed Dr. Grenfell. Then he heard about the great need for doctors among the poor fishermen in cold Labrador. This door bids us to go out again to our work. Jesus said to Dr. Grenfell, " Go to Labrador to help the sick."

No wonder Jesus said, " I am the door." We come into this church by this door, and we go out by it. So, also, we come to God by Jesus, and we go out into the world by Jesus to work for God.

28

THE GOOD SHEPHERD

Object: A shepherd's crook. (A cane may be used.)

Story: A farmer was walking over his farm with a friend. He showed the friend his fields of grain, his herds of cattle and flocks of sheep. The friend was especially interested in the sheep. He had seen the same breed before, but never such big, healthy-looking animals. He asked the farmer how he succeeded in raising such splendid sheep. The farmer answered, " I take care of my lambs, my friend."

In the first verse of Psalm 23 we read, " The Lord is my shepherd." A shepherd is a man who takes care of lambs and sheep. How does he do this?

Taking care of flocks of sheep has always been one of the main occupations in Palestine. This was true in Old Testament times and continues to this day. The shepherd in Palestine leads his sheep into rough, mountainous country in search of grass. Because of the wildness of the land, we find many wild animals there, and therefore the shepherd must protect his sheep. The shepherd leads his sheep and they follow him. In his hand he carries his only weapon, a staff, such as I am holding in my hand. Of course, the staff of the shepherd is much longer, almost as tall as the shepherd himself, and much more crudely formed. Sometimes it is made from a branch with a tree root attached. All the shoots are cut from the root, leaving only a round ball into which the shepherd drives nails or attaches a piece of iron.

This staff he uses for several purposes. While leading the way he has a trusty stick to aid him in climbing steep mountains. The staff helps him get a foothold. With it he can dislodge rocks which are in his way, and when he is tired he can lean upon it to rest. Also, with the crook he can rescue his sheep from danger. If he sees a sheep getting too near the edge of a precipice he catches one of his hind legs in the crook and gently pulls it back and then restores it to the rest of the flock. Then, again, he can use it for protection. When a wild animal prowls about the place where the sheep lie in the nightime, the shepherd uses the other, the heavy iron-tipped end to strike him such a blow that he runs away howling. So you see, the staff is of great use to the shepherd in his care of the sheep.

Our text reads, " The Lord is my shepherd." The Psalmist compares the Lord to a shepherd, so we, therefore, must be the sheep and the lambs. As a shepherd cares for his sheep, so the Lord cares for us. A shepherd leads the way, and the Lord shows us the way to go, and we should follow Him. The shepherd removes some of the rocks with his staff to make the way easier. So also the way is made easier for us when we follow Christ, the Good Shepherd.

When a sheep gets too near the edge of a precipice, the shepherd pulls him out of danger. So God, when we wander from the straight way, calls us to return to follow in His footsteps. As the shepherd protects his sheep from wild beasts, so the Lord protects us from evil if we but trust in Him. All He asks of us is, " Follow me."

In the Great Mammoth Cave of Kentucky there are caves opening one into the other. There is nothing but darkness in the great cave, except when someone brings in artificial light. Every little while the words, " Keep close to your guide," come to the ears of the people who are being shown the cave. That is what we must do if we would pass safely through the dangerous places in life. Remember, " The Lord is my shepherd." Keep close to your Guide.

29

GOD ANSWERS PRAYER

Object: A ball of cord, in a box with a cover which has a hole in it through which to pull the string.

Story: In the town of Kamajura in Japan there is an immense statue of Buddha. We often see reproductions of this statue in the form of incense-burners. This statue of Buddha is a majestic figure seated with arms folded and a look of peace and calm upon his face. His eyes are closed; there is an air of indifference about him, as if he did not care what was happening in the world around him. His attitude seems to say, " Let me sit by the side of the road and let the world go by." Of what use is a God like that who does not care what happens to his followers?

Now let us turn our eyes to the real God. Does He in any way resemble Buddha? In Psalm 46: 1 we read, " God is our refuge and strength, a very present help in trouble." Our God is not sitting down, He is keeping watch above His own. His arms are not folded, for in the Book of Deuteronomy we read, " The eternal God is thy refuge and underneath are the everlasting arms." They are stretched out to help us in the hour of need.

A great many years ago, according to an Arabian legend, there lived in the city of Bagdad a much respected citizen named Sinbad the sailor. I am sure most of you have read about him. He had been a great traveler and had become famous on account of his wonderful adventures. Several times he lost all his possessions and more than once his life was threatened. But after each disaster he returned to his home in safety, richer than when he had departed. He spent his evenings in telling stories of his wonderful escapes, which he attributed to God, who was always there ready to help him in the time of trouble. " Faith in God," he said, " is our strength in time of need."

Sometime ago, a United States Navy plane ran out of gasoline in mid-Pacific. There was nothing to do but land in the water. The plane sank, but three of the crew managed to inflate a four-by-eight-foot rubber raft and crawl aboard. They saved no food or water, nothing but a pistol, knife, and a pair of pliers.

Here stands a box in which there is a ball of cord. This ball of cord represents a person's span of life— the years, months, and days he will live. We do not know how long the cord in this box is, neither do we know how long our life will be. The three wrecked men on the raft wondered whether their days were numbered, whether they were almost at the end of the ball of cord. (At various intervals of your talk pull out lengths of cord.)

At the end of five days the lack of water bothered the men. They knew that if they had no rain they would soon die of thirst. Gene, the youngest man, suggested that they should pray for help. So they held their first daily prayer meeting. Hardly had they stopped praying when the rain came and they had their first drink in five days. More days passed. Was their span of life almost ended? (Pull out more cord.) Again they prayed to God for more rain and food, and also sang hymns. Next morning Gene killed a fish by stabbing it with the penknife. The days went on (more cord), and each morning they wondered whether that day would be the end. Then a bird landed on the boat and Gene shot it. Again they had food. Day after day they prayed to God for help and asked Him to save them.

Our ball of cord is getting smaller. I wonder whether we are almost at the end. That is what the three men on the raft thought. They wondered if they were almost at the end of their lives. The days are slowly passing. " O God," prayed the men, " bring us safely to shore." On the twenty-ninth day the men began to feel hopeless. They felt that the end of their life must be near, but still they looked to God in prayer. (More cord.) The morning of the thirty-fourth day was clear. Suddenly they see the shore line of an island and know that they are saved. For thirty-four days it seemed that their cord of life might come to an end at any time. But God had been their refuge and strength. (Now take ball of cord from box.) See, there is still much cord left. God had saved their lives.

We need never fear, although we may think that the end of life (the end of the cord) is near. God is always here. He will never forsake us. He is ever present, "keeping watch above His own."

30

THE PRICE OF PERFECTION

Object: A colorful piece of pottery.

Story: Before (hold up pottery) this became a beautiful vase it was nothing but a lump of clay. There is a story told about a vase which I must tell you. The potter took clay into his hands and with the aid of the potter's wheel (an instrument in the form of a wheel which helps the potter shape the clay) he formed the shapeless piece of clay into a vase. The potter said, "The shape is perfect." Then he called his servant and told him to put the vase into the oven. The heat of the furnace became intense, and the vase said to itself, "The master potter said that I was perfect; why then must I endure this heat?" At last the fire had done its work, and the potter looked at the vase and again said that it was perfect. But the vase was not yet finished. Now it was covered with enamel, and once more it was subjected to terrific heat. When it came from the oven it was pure white.

Surely, now all the painful processes were over. But, no, the master potter then began to color it. Again it was put into the oven and the color was burned on the vase. Once more the potter said, " It is perfect." However, it was not yet completed. The potter traced on it a design, and the vase once again was baked at a much higher temperature. Then it was taken from the fire. The master potter was satisfied and said, " It is finished; it is perfect." Looking at this vase, we can also say, " It is finished; it is perfect."

One evening a young boy named Joseph went to a concert. He watched the pianist and listened to his wonderful music. Sometimes it seemed to speak of thunder, then like falling rain; sometimes the music was light and gay and spoke of happiness; then it became calm and sad, and finally came the climax, a note of triumph. " Oh," thought Joseph, " I wish I could become a musician like that! " After the concert was over, he went to the pianist and said, " How can I learn to play the piano like that? "

This was the answer he received: " Joseph, it takes many, many years, much patience and hard work and sacrifices without number to become an accomplished pianist. I will tell you my experience. While I was in public school, I had to practice four hours every day after school. The other boys would call, ' Come out. Let's go coasting or play hide-and-seek.' But I had to apply myself to my music. When I got into high school, still my music had to come first. No playing baseball, basketball or football. I had no time for them, and also I had to be careful not to harm my hands. In college there were still more distractions, but I had to keep my face set toward my goal. After all these years of preparation, tonight has been my first concert. If you want to be an exceptional pianist you must be prepared to work hard and endure sacrifices and hardships."

You see it is not easy to attain perfection. The vase had to endure intense heat again and again before it became perfect. The pianist had to spend years of practice and sacrifice before he attained his wonderful playing.

If we want to live a truly Christian life it is not easy. It is not enough to say, " Yes, I want to be a Christian; I want to be like Jesus and I want to join the church." That is only the beginning. Like the vase, you have just been formed, and, like the musician, you have just started playing your scales. Now, comes the time of preparation.

You try to practice the Christ way of living. Illness comes upon you; you are impatient to be well, like the vase enduring heat and the musician with his hours of practice each day. Your illness has taught you a lesson, the art of patience. Christ was patient and He wants you to be patient. Someone has wronged you, but Christ practiced the Golden Rule, so you must do unto others as you would have others do unto you. Then you learn Christ's rule for kindness. And thus it goes, and we learn that it takes much practice to be a good Christian. Let us remember that the vase was not made beautiful and perfect at one time, and that the musician had to do much practicing before he could give his first concert. It is the same way in being a Christian. The vase had to endure much heat, which it did not like. When things come into our lives which we do not like, that is the time to practice being Christian. With much practice we will become more perfect.

31

CARBON COPIES OF JESUS

Objects: Two sheets of typewriter paper. One sheet of carbon paper.

Story: If I put this piece of carbon paper between these two sheets of typewriter paper and use this pencil to write the word " Jesus " on the top sheet, what occurs? Yes, you are right. If I look at the sheet of paper beneath the carbon paper I will see the word " Jesus." It is a carbon copy of the original sheet, almost as plain and distinct as the word on the first sheet. I have here, then, a carbon copy of the word " Jesus." A carbon copy is an image, a likeness of the real thing. Don't you think that it would be a good idea to be a carbon copy of Jesus? I know we would all like to copy Jesus, but how can we do it?

Paul writing to the early Christians speaks of " looking unto Jesus," and of being " transformed into the same image." In our own words we might say, " We can become carbon copies of Jesus by looking up to Him."

There is an old legend about a prince who had a crooked back. He was very sensitive about this affliction. So he asked the best sculptor in his kingdom to make a statue of him with a straight back. When the statue was finished, the prince had it placed in a secret nook in his garden. Every day he would go into this hidden place and gaze long and earnestly at the statue. Months passed and people began to notice that the prince's back was not so crooked as it had been and that he seemed much nobler looking. The prince went into the garden once more and looked earnestly at the statue and then at himself, and, lo, his back had grown as straight as the perfect statue. He had become a carbon copy of the statue.

If we desire to be a carbon copy of Jesus we must keep in daily contact with Him, never taking our eyes from the ideal we wish to attain.

Two boys were playing in the snow one day. They decided to see who could make the straightest path in the snow. One boy fixed his eyes on a tree and walked toward it without once taking his eyes off the goal. The other boy, too, used the same tree for an objective, but when he had gone a short distance he turned around to see how straight his path was. He walked on a little further and again turned around to investigate. When they arrived at their destination they stopped and looked back. One path was straight as an arrow, while the other was filled with zigzags. The first boy kept his eyes on the tree until he reached it, while the other stopped, looked back, and wandered from his course.

If we fix our eyes upon Jesus and continually keep them there we will become true carbon copies of Him. However, if our eyes wander here and there and we get off our course our carbon copy will be smudged and blurred. If we want to be " transformed into the same image " we must look unto Jesus.

This carbon copy is like the original on which we

wrote the name Jesus. Jesus is God's original man, of whom we are to be carbon copies. God wants us to be like Jesus. He is the perfect man for us to copy. We are by no means perfect. There are so many things wrong with us. When we ask what would Jesus do if He were I, we would be copying Him. Jesus was kind, loving, helpful, reverent, and He loved God and His neighbor. He never sinned. He lived the good life. That is what we should try to do. Let us do our best to be carbon copies of Him.

32

A SMALL BEGINNING

Object: A kernel of corn or wheat.

Story: A kernel of corn—what a small, insignificant grain it seems to be! What can we do with just one kernel? We might throw it away or feed it to the chickens, for, after all, one kernel has not much value. However, we could plant it, and what would the result be? It will produce a cornstalk on which we will have at least one ear of corn. On this ear we will find many kernels. Suppose we should plant all those kernels next year. Then in the fall we could harvest hundreds of ears of corn. These hundreds of ears would have thousands and thousands of kernels, and if these should be planted, our harvest would be tremendous. From this one original grain of corn would come millions of bushels. If we continued this for many years it would be impossible to calculate the result.

Almost two thousand years ago there was born in

Bethlehem of Judea, in the country of Palestine, a baby who was called Jesus. What can a small baby do? When He was thirty years of age He became a teacher. He taught men in that far-away country of Palestine, a small land only as large as our state of Connecticut, about God the Father and how to live the right kind of a life. He planted the seed of Christianity. He called twelve men, whom we know as disciples, to follow Him. After only three years of teaching, He was crucified. What happened to the seed He had planted?

There is a legend that when Jesus left this earth and returned to heaven, the angel Gabriel came to Him and said, " What will happen to the work you have started on earth? " Jesus answered, " Gabriel, I have left my twelve disciples on earth and I am depending on them." Let us see whether these men remained faithful to the trust that Jesus placed in them and continued sowing the seeds of Christianity. Less than thirty years after the death of Jesus, growing Christian communities were to be found in all the important cities of the eastern and northern Mediterranean.

How did this happen? In those days there lived a young man named Paul. He was a doctor of the law and was very much opposed to the teachings of Jesus. He was appointed to stamp out Christianity, but when he saw what good its teachings were accomplishing he became its champion. And what a champion he became! Instead of Christianity being established only in little Palestine, it was planted in many parts of the world by the missionary Paul.

We saw what a large crop of corn can come from this one kernel. So Christianity was started by Jesus and planted by His disciples. Other disciples planted it, and still more disciples planted it. From one kernel planted by Jesus Christ Christianity grew until it became the religion of the entire then known world. Soon steeples and towers of churches began to dot the hills and valleys of Europe. Christianity was growing.

Then it was brought to our country, America, by the Pilgrims, the Quakers, the Moravians, the Dutch, the Swedes, the Spaniards, the Germans, and others. From these original colonies it was carried across our entire continent. The seeds of Christianity were multiplying.

Still, it needed more fields. So about a hundred and fifty years ago, missionaries, people who carry the teachings of Jesus to places where they are not known, went to lands far away. Ever since they have gone to India, Africa, China, Japan, Arabia, and every other country on our earth. Kernels of Christianity have been planted in every one of them.

From a small beginning started by one person, Jesus, in one small country, Christianity has gone into every part of the world.

Is our planting finished? No! We must continue until every man, woman and child in every country on the globe acknowledges Jesus as the Christ and Christianity as their religion.

33

TALKING HANDS

Object: The hand.

Story: Our text today is found in Ecclesiastes 9: 10, " Whatsoever thy hand findeth to do, do it with thy might." The hand has been called the most wonderful tool in the world. It never refuses to work for us. It is always obedient; it does just what we tell it to do.

Good hands are those that are busy with work that is honest and true. Rudyard Kipling wrote:

> " There's not a hand so weak and white, nor yet a
>   heart so sick,
>   But it can find some needful job that's crying
>   to be done."

Our text states, " Whatsoever thy hand findeth to do, do it with thy might." In connection with the National Children's Home and Orphanage in England, which cares for thousands of children who have no home, there has been formed a St. Christopher's League. It is a league of boys and girls ready to lend a hand to unfortunate children. St. Christopher, who in the Middle Ages built his hut near a river ford and in time of flood carried people and especially children across, is their ideal. In their own way they are trying to help as he helped, setting aside part of their time or skill in the service of others who need a helper. Jesus helped wherever He was needed, healing the sick and curing the lame. We, too, should be helpers, keeping our hands busy, doing the tasks that we can perform to the best of our ability. There is an old proverb which tells us that the devil finds work for idle hands. This means that if we are not busy in good work we get into mischief.

Let us examine the hand more closely. Look at it now (hold up fist). It is clenched in a fist. It is raised in anger; it shows a fighting spirit. Is it wrong for us to be angry? Was Jesus ever angry? If we study the New Testament we will find that the only time Jesus showed anger was against sin. Do you remember the story of how Jesus drove the money-changers out of the temple? Jesus was justly angry because they misused the church. Whenever we come across wrong, dishonesty, bad language, and idle gossip, we have a right to be angry and clench our fists. Often we are angry when we have no right to be angry. When something does not suit us, if we do not feel well, when things go against us, if we are unable to get our arithmetic problems, or we have no money to buy a soda, then we are angry with ourselves and others. We have no right to that kind of anger. That is what we call a bad temper or a bad disposition. But, like Jesus, we have a right to be angry when we see sin and evil. Then we may clench our fists.

Slowly I open my fist and my hand opens to show a grasping action. The fingers look like claws; they look ugly and almost make us shudder. Grasping fingers like these show a greedy and selfish person. Such a person is thinking only of himself and what he can " rake in " with his clawlike fingers. It is said that in Japan there is a bird which has but one note, " Me! Me! Me! " Some American people visiting there called it " the me bird." When we hold out a hand in a grasping action we are like the " me bird "; all we think about is ourselves. Greedy and selfish people have no friends and are unhappy.

Let us turn the hand, palm upward. What a change! It now seems to say, " I want to be friendly; I want to welcome you." One day a number of little children wanted to come to Jesus. His disciples tried to prevent this, but Jesus turned around, held out His hand and said, " Let the little children come unto me." Jesus was friendly. Sometimes a new girl or boy moves into our community. Be friendly. Go to him, bid him welcome, and take him to church and school with you. Not only will the little stranger feel at home, but you will feel that the welcoming gesture has made you happy. If we want friends we must be friends.

The index finger of the hand is used for pointing. Along the road we often see signs in the form of a hand with the index finger pointing the way we are to go. What is the right way to live? Is there anyone pointing out the right way for us? Yes, there is. Jesus points out the right way for us. He said, " I am the way." He directs us along the right way of life. And we can help others to live right by pointing them to Jesus. A prisoner asked the apostle Paul what he had to do to be saved. He wanted to know the way. Paul said, " Believe on the Lord Jesus Christ." We, too, must point to Jesus.

What we do with our hands pretty well shows what we are thinking about. Let us thank God for hands.

34

DAILY WINDING

Object: Alarm clock.

Story: A man, a woman, a boy, or girl, is like an alarm clock in many respects. In an ordinary clock there are over two hundred parts, while in the human body there are still more. A clock is wonderfully made, but a man is much more wonderful and could have been made only by God. No wonder the Psalmist said in Psalm 139, verse 14: " For I am fearfully and wonderfully made."

As we look at the clock, the first thing we notice are

the hands. The hands indicate the time. In the village square there stood a large clock. Everyone in the community was in the habit of setting his watches and clocks by it. One day the clock was thirty minutes slow. As Mr. James walked by the clock he said to himself, " I am early this morning, I'll take my time." But he was late for work. On her way to school, Edna looked at the clock and sauntered along slowly, so she was tardy. Mrs. Park, who lived near the Square, did not have dinner ready when her family came home, for she depended on the clock. So many people were late because the clock upon which they depended misled them. We, too, have hands, and others are watching to see how we use them. The Bible says, " Whatsoever thy hand findeth to do, do it with thy might." This means that our hands should be busy doing something useful. I know of an old mother whose hands are calloused and worn and her fingers gnarly from much work for her family and others. Those are good hands. They have always set a good example for others. They are not like the hands of the slow clock that misled the people in the village. If your hands are idle, others will say, " He is lazy, I can be lazy too."

This clock has an alarm. When the alarm rings in the morning it says, " Time to get up." Sometimes we try to ignore it and we bury our head in the pillow to shut out the sound. But the alarm gets louder and louder, and, finally, we obey its summons. We also have an alarm in us. It is called conscience. It expects obedience from us. Robert was on his way to Young People's meeting. He passed by the movie theater. It seemed to beckon to him and say, " Robert, come in and see the exciting picture. Your parents won't know that you have not gone to church." Robert almost yielded to the temptation, but his alarm, his conscience, kept on ringing and saying, " You must attend Young People's meeting. You can go to the theater during the week." Robert heeded the warning of his conscience and went on to church. We too, like Robert, need an alarm, a conscience, to warn us to do what is right.

For the clock to run well the works must be kept clean. We must not drop it or expose the works to the air, which is filled with dust. Then our clock must be taken to the jeweler to be fixed. So our thoughts must be kept clean and right. Then our deeds will be good. We must guard our thinking so no evil can enter our minds. Bad companions may seem attractive, but if their ideas enter our minds they pollute us. Our minds, as well as the clock, can get dirty. If we are not careful the evil may become uppermost in our minds. When this happens we need to go to the Jeweler. The only Jeweler that can clean our hearts and minds is God. He can give us good thoughts for bad ones, love for hate, and kindness for anger.

The mainspring is well named, for it is the most important part of the clock. It is the power that keeps the wheels moving. If it is out of order, the clock stops. We, too, have a mainspring; it is our soul. The mainspring in this clock must be wound every day to keep it going. Thus it is with our souls; we have to go to God every day. Every day we need winding up by God, just as the clock needs daily winding. When we go to Sunday school, to church, to Young People's meeting, and to our own rooms to pray, we are winding the mainspring, our soul. We receive power from God. The power in the mainspring makes the clock keep perfect time. The power of God in our souls makes us live right.

35

WE LIVE AGAIN
(Easter)

Object: A potato.

Story: Potatoes like this one are a common food on all our tables. A dinner would hardly be complete without them. Since so many potatoes are eaten, the farmers must raise large crops of them.

We know that everything that grows comes from a seed, root, or bulb, which must have life in it in order to grow. If we plant this potato it will grow. A tender sprout would soon appear above the ground, then this would develop into a plant with many leaves. After a while there would be new potatoes from this one. So we know that there is life in this potato. I wonder whether we could find that life. Let us search for it.

I will take this knife and cut it in half. We examine each part but are unable to find life. We will cut it up into smaller pieces and look each piece over carefully. Still, I am not able to find the life that I know is in it.

In this way man is very much like a potato. Man has a soul. If we could take man apart, do you think that we could find out where the soul is? Do you think that we could see the soul? We took the potato apart, but we could not see the life that is in it. Neither can you see the soul, but it is there. Once a doctor and a minister were arguing about the soul. The doctor said that there is no soul. The minister contradicted him and said, " There is a soul."

Finally, the doctor said, " Did you ever see your soul? "

" No," said the minister.

" Then," said the doctor, " you have no soul; I believe only in the things that I can see."

" Now, let me ask you a question," said the minister. " Did you ever have a pain? "

" Why, of course," replied the doctor.

" Did you see the pain? " asked the minister.

" No," admitted the doctor.

" Then you did not have a pain," said the minister, " because you said you believed only in the things that you could see."

You cannot see a pain, but when you have hit your finger with a hammer you know that it is there. You cannot see the life in the potato, but it is there and it will grow. Although we cannot see the soul, we know it is there, because we can feel it.

It is the soul, that part of us which we cannot see, which lives on in the next world, even though our bodies die. That is what Easter means. The body dies, but the most important part of us, our soul, lives on. If we put this potato into the ground it will grow into a very nice green plant. And as you see the plant you wonder what happened to the potato. So you dig under the plant, you tunnel under it to see if you can find it. Will you find it? No! The old potato is gone, but the life that was in it, which we could not find, lives on in the plant.

So it is with us. Our bodies die but our souls live on. Easter tells us that this is true. As you know, Jesus was crucified. Then His disciples came to put His body in a tomb. Jesus was dead; they had buried Him. But on the third day, the day we call Easter,

He arose and was very much alive. He lived again.
Was only Jesus to live again? No indeed, and that
is what makes Easter such a happy day. Jesus as-
sured us that because He lived again we too shall live.

36

THE DIRECTION-FINDER

Objects: A compass and a Bible.

Story: This interesting object is called a compass. We
find one on every ship. Many travelers carry one.
They are very useful objects. Why does a ship need a
compass and a traveler often carry one? What can a
little instrument like this do? It directs the sailor
and the traveler to their destinations. Without it they
would be lost. If there is no path through the ocean
or the woods the sailor and traveler have no guide to
lead the way.

It seems strange that a small instrument like this
compass can be a guide. Let us examine it more
closely. Looking through the glass, we see a needle
evenly balanced on a pivot, and on the face are marked
the directions, north, south, east, and west. The needle,
being a magnet, always points in one direction, north.
The North Pole attracts it, and, no matter where you
may be, the needle of the compass always points to
the north. So the traveler never gets lost in directions.
The compass is always a safe guide on land or on the
ocean.

Likewise, we need a safe guide for our daily life.
Where shall we get such a safe guide? The answer is

the Bible. As the compass points to the North Pole, so the Bible always points to God. With the Bible as our guide we shall always know what is right. A pilot on a ship with the needle of the compass pointing to the north is never lost. So a man with the Bible pointing toward God is never lost but is always going in the right direction.

Let us look into the Bible to see how it points out the right way just as the compass needle always points in the right direction. In Exodus, chapter twenty, we find the Ten Commandments. These are laws that guide us in our daily life. Not only do they show us in what direction to go, but all the laws of our country are based on them. These Ten Commandments are also the foundation of the code of laws in every civilized country. God not only gave these to the Israelites thousands of years ago, but He meant them also for us and for everyone on earth. The Ten Commandments point out the right way to live.

We will turn the pages of our Bible to one of the greatest verses in the Old Testament. In the sixth chapter and the eighth verse of Micah we read, " What doth the Lord require of thee, but to do justly, to love mercy and to walk humbly with thy God? " Here God points to three things we should do: always do right, be kind, and be not proud. If we do this we are going in the right direction.

Then, in the New Testament we come to the teachings of Jesus. In the fifth chapter of Matthew we find the Beatitudes. Here Jesus tells us that we will be " blessed " if we do this and that, and if we are the kind of people He wants us to be. Blessed means to be very happy. We all want to be happy. Read the Beatitudes and see for yourself how Jesus points the way to happiness. The Bible always points in the right direction, just as the compass does.

The " Great Commandment " was given to us by Jesus. In Matthew twenty-two, verses thirty-seven to forty, we read, " Thou shalt love the Lord thy God with all thy heart, and with all thy soul, and with all thy mind, and with all thy strength. This is the first and great commandment. And the second is like unto it, Thou shalt love thy neighbor as thyself. On these two commandments hang all the law and the prophets." Jesus asks us first to love God and then our neighbor. If we do this we certainly cannot go wrong. The Bible never steers us wrong. It always shows us the right way in which to go.

Remember (hold up compass), the needle of the compass always points in one direction. If we follow it we will arrive at our destination. The Bible (hold up Bible) also points in one direction toward God; if we follow it, it will guide us safely through life.

37

THE BEST IN US

Object: A bottle of milk.

Story: This (holding up bottle of milk) is a very common object in all of our homes. We use it every day. Do you think such an ordinary, everyday object can teach us a lesson? As we look at this bottle of milk we see that the upper part of the milk has a slightly different color from the rest. That is the cream which has risen to the top, the best part of the milk.

Have you ever heard the expression, "the cream of the crop"? One day, when Janet was out in the rose garden, her mother pointed to a beautiful red rose and said, "Janet, that is the cream of the crop." She meant that it was the loveliest rose of all. When a farmer wants seed corn for planting, he looks over many ears of corn and selects the largest, longest, and fullest ears. In other words, he picks out the "cream of the crop." If he does this he will have a good crop of corn the next year.

Looking at this milk, we see that the best, the cream, rises to the top. That is exactly what should happen in our lives. The best in us should rise to the top. How can the best in us come to the top?

The Bible says that as a man thinks in his heart so is he. Once upon a time there was a boy who was always mean and cruel to others. At school he teased and tormented smaller boys and at home he slapped his little sister. He loved to catch flies, tear off their wings and then watch them try to fly. He got worse and worse as he grew older, and, finally, he became so wicked that he was put into prison. He started by thinking of plans to tease others and gradually all the bad came to the top. How sad! He became wicked because he always thought about wickedness.

But suppose, instead of thinking about plans to tease others, this boy had thought good thoughts. If he had been kind and gentle to the smaller boys at school and to his little sister, goodness would have showed in his dealings with others. As he thought about ways of helpfulness, cruel and wicked ideas would have been crowded out and goodness and kindness would have risen to the top like the cream on the milk. As the years went on he would have grown into a man who was looked up to and respected. For as a man thinks in his heart so is he.

Also, we must allow only the best to come to the top in thinking of others. You know, Jesus always tried to find the best in everyone. In those days tax collectors were much hated men because of their greediness. They collected the taxes for Rome, which at that time was ruling Palestine. Suppose the government assessed you $100 for taxes. The tax collector would come to you and say, " John, your taxes are $125, pay me or I'll take away your property." You see, the tax collector tried to squeeze as much money out of the people as possible, for whatever amount he got over the government's assessment belonged to him. Matthew was one of those tax collectors. One day Jesus saw him collecting taxes and called to him, " Matthew, follow me." Matthew left his business and followed Jesus. Others saw only evil in him, but Jesus saw the good. Matthew became one of Jesus' twelve disciples and he wrote the first book in the New Testament. As Jesus saw good in Matthew, we also ought to look for the best in others. If we do this, the best will always come to the top in others.

How can the best come to the top in our lives? If we shake the milk in this bottle and stir it up, the cream, the best, would no longer be at the top. If our lives are constantly stirred up in busyness and excitement the best in us has no opportunity to show itself. Our lives need a period of calmness and quiet. Jesus needed times like that. We remember that He often went for hours and sometimes for days to a quiet place to talk to His heavenly Father. We need a quiet time for reading our Bible and for the worship of God. When we pray and worship, we cannot think evil but only the best, and so only the best in us will have an opportunity to rise to the top, just as the cream will rise to the top of the milk if it stands quietly.

38

LIGHT AND POWER
(An Outdoor Meeting)

Object: A campfire.

Story: The sun has set, day is dying in the west, and the stars are beginning to peep forth, one by one. A deep silence covers the earth. Darkness has come. Can we dispel this darkness? This campfire gives us light.

How did we start this fire? First of all, we took some small twigs, then some larger branches, and, finally, several big logs. But the fire itself was started with a small match.

I see two things in this fire. They are power and light. Let us talk first about power in the fire. In it there is a power for good and one for bad. Did you know that man has been called " the fire-using animal "? He uses fire to clear the ground for farming, and he burns up weeds and refuse. Fire heats our homes, it keeps us warm, and cooks our food. It is a good power.

But through man's carelessness it causes much destruction. A carelessly tossed match starts a big fire. One man-caused fire swept over 90,000 acres of Glacier National Park and left a " graveyard " of blackened stumps. Man, " the fire-using animal," has used fire for good and evil.

What starts this fire? A match, a spark, and then it begins to burn; more fuel is added, and the fire burns more powerfully. Little by little, it grows bigger and bigger. Every fire has a small beginning. So it is in our lives. A child finds a penny on the floor in his home. He thinks, " I'll keep it; it is such a small coin, no one will miss it." A year later he is not only keeping the pennies but taking dimes from his mother's purse. As he grows older, the sums grow larger, and one day, when he is a grown man, he robs a bank of thousands of dollars. A penny was only a small thing, a spark, but through it the child started to steal, and at last the small thing became so great that it overwhelmed him and landed him in prison. A little wrong has become a great evil.

However, a spark also can grow to be a great power for good. At the beginning of the nineteenth century there lived in England a young girl named Florence Nightingale. In those days there were very few nurses and those were ignorant. Florence decided to become a nurse, for she loved to care for sick people. In 1854 war broke out between England and Russia, called the Crimean War. After the battles, wounded men were brought in from the front and left to suffer and to die, for there was no one, no trained nurse, to care for them properly. When Florence Nightingale heard this, she got together a group of thirty-eight women to go to Crimea to care for the wounded. She stayed there until the war was over and then returned to her home in England. Her influence led to the organization of the Red Cross. Only a spark, one young woman who loved nursing, but it kindled a big fire, for out of it grew the Red Cross, which is now a worldwide organization, a great power for good.

The fire is not only a power, it is also a light. Our bonfire tonight throws a big circle of light around us. Suppose someone were lost in this dark woods tonight. That person would look around in all directions and in the distance he would discover a faint gleam from this fire. Setting his face toward that gleam of light, he would walk directly toward it and finally arrive here at the bonfire. Only a faint gleam but it has led him to safety. As the fire is a light, so Jesus Christ is our Light in this world. He said, "I am the light of the world." His light is shining today, and if we would be safe we must follow it. With Him we are never lost. He guides us safely in this world and into the next.

39

THE BEST SELLER

Object: The Bible.

Story: The world is full of books, some good and others bad. But in my hand I hold the best book of all, the Bible. How did we get this wonderful book? Why is it the best seller of all times? In what way can the Bible help us? Let us try to find answers to these questions.

First, how did we get this wonderful book? (Hold up Bible.) In it are sixty-six books written by at least forty men. These men were shepherds, fishermen, doctors, kings, peasants, educated and uneducated. It took them over a thousand years to write it. In it are history, biography, poetry, philosophy, and letters, all put together to form one book, the Bible.

Some of our mothers have books about their children. In them we find pictures from babyhood to manhood. The first pictures are those of the baby, then one of the child learning to walk, others of the child growing up, then some of the youth, and, finally, several of the grown-up man. All different but all the same person. So this Bible, from beginning to end, is the Story of God.

More than fifteen hundred years ago all these sixty-six books were collected into one volume which we call the Bible. We have had our English Bible for about four hundred years. Other very old books, and even most books written fifty years ago, have been forgotten. But the Bible never grows old; it fits the conditions in the world today just as it did thousands of years ago.

Now we come to our second question, Why is it the best seller? The Bible has been translated into more than a thousand languages and dialects. It is found all over the world. It has the place of honor in the homes of the poor as well as the rich. Other books have been written for certain peoples, but the Bible is for every land and race. Children can understand it and adults study it. It contains the world's best literature. For hundreds of years it has been the standard of English for everyone. In it we also find the Ten Commandments, upon which all the laws of the country are based. All our better books and magazines refer again and again to the Bible. Men, like Columbus, were guided by the Bible. From the topmost mast on his ship, the *Pinta*, floated a banner with the words, " In the Name of Jesus."

Yes, the Bible is a best seller. Since this is true, we come to our third question: In what way can it help us? We should not only buy a copy of the Bible but also use it. A young girl once was asked whether her family had a Bible. She answered, " Yes, that's where we keep our newspaper clippings." Our Bible should be a guide to show us how to live. The compass has a needle which always points north, so we always know in what direction we are going. The Bible is a compass; it shows us how to live. If we follow it we will have a prosperous journey through life.

Men and women have done their greatest work through the influence of the Bible. It inspires the pictures of great artists, and the grandest music is based upon the stories of the Bible. When miners go down into the mine they wear a lamp called the " Davy lamp " on their caps. This lights their way in the dark mine. So the Bible is a lamp that lights our way in this world. As the Psalmist has said, " Thy word (hold up Bible) is a lamp unto my feet and a light unto my path."

40

OUR COUNTRY
(Patriotic)

Object: The seal of the United States of America. (This may be found on a dollar bill.)

Story: More than one hundred fifty years ago, when George Washington was President, Congress approved a design for a national coat-of-arms, a copy of which I hold in my hand. It also is called the Seal of the United States of America. Let us examine this emblem more closely.

The eagle is the first object our eyes discover. But why does an eagle represent our country? Of all the birds that fly, the eagle is to us the most interesting. It has been thus in all ages and in all lands. The eagle has been an inspiration to poets and other writers. He is mentioned many times in our Bible. In him are combined strength and swiftness. Looking at him, we say, "Yes, he is the king of the birds."

The early Romans carried eagles into battle. In their camps they built chapels for the eagles, and the soldiers worshiped them because of their strength and dignity. So through the ages he came to be looked upon as a symbol of greatness.

Therefore, when our Congress looked for an idea for a seal, they chose the bald or American eagle. He is called a bald eagle because the feathers about his head are white in contrast with his dark body, so that from a distance he looks bald. The bald eagle is found in every one of our states. He is American. He is strong, as our country must be strong. An adult eagle has a wing-spread of from seven to eight feet. These large, strong wings give him the freedom of the air, for they carry him swiftly and surely. The eagle, then, is American, is strong and free. As the eagle is strong and free, so our country is strong and free.

Let us look at the seal once more. We see that the eagle is holding something in his bill. It is a scroll. This scroll is inscribed with a motto, *E Pluribus Unum,* which means "One out of many." What a strange motto that is! It has a wonderful meaning. We are one nation but many states. From many states we have formed one strong nation, "one out of many." Suppose I had a number of sticks. I could easily break them one by one. But now I will make one bundle out of these sticks. If I should try to break that bundle it would not be possible. From many weak sticks I have made one strong bundle. From many weak states we have formed one strong nation. Now we understand our motto found on the scroll in the beak of the eagle *E Pluribus Unum,* or " One out of many."

Again we look at the seal. In the left talon of the eagle we find thirteen arrows. These thirteen arrows represent the thirteen original colonies. If our country is in danger, all colonies, all states, not just one, defend the land we love. The arrows mean that we will fight if we must.

The eagle (looking at the seal) also has something in his right talon. It looks like the small branch of a tree. It is an olive branch. Why should there be an olive branch on our seal? An olive branch has become the emblem of peace; our country on its seal shows that we are a peace-loving nation.

There was a dispute about the boundary line between Chile and Argentina, two countries in South America. The people in both countries started to prepare for war. This happened during Easter week. On Easter morning people came to church to worship. Bishop Benavente spoke some startling words: " We have come to worship Christ the Prince of Peace. But we have forgotten what He taught. We hate our neighbors and plan to fight them. Let us live in peace, as Christ taught us." The news of this sermon spread over both countries. People finally decided to take their guns and weapons of war and mold them into a statue of Christ and to erect this statue on the mountains between the two countries. On the statue are inscribed these words, " These mountains will crumble into dust sooner than the people of Argentina and of Chile will break the peace which at the feet of Christ the Redeemer they have given their word to keep." To these people Christ symbolizes peace. As we look at this olive branch, the emblem of peace, we are reminded of Christ, the author of peace.

The eagle on our seal shows us that our country is strong and free, that the forty-eight states make one strong nation, that we will fight only if we must, and that we hope and desire peace.

41

ABRAHAM LINCOLN

Object: A penny.

Story: Can you all see what I have in my hand? It is a penny. If you have one in your pocket or purse please take it out and look at it. Of course, the first thing we notice is the picture of Abraham Lincoln. He was one of our greatest presidents, was he not? I wonder why we find the picture of the most beloved president on the smallest, the least valuable, coin which we have in our country? I think it is because there are more pennies in circulation than any other coin. When we see a penny we are reminded again and again of him whose picture we see on it, Abraham Lincoln.

Just above his picture we read four words, " In God We Trust." These words are found not only on pennies but also on nickels, dimes, quarters, half dollars, and silver dollars. Everyone should put his trust in God. These words, " In God We Trust," seem to fit

Lincoln especially. One day he said to his friend Mr. Brooks, " I would be the veriest blockhead if I should try to get through a single day of business without relying on Him who doeth all things well."

A visitor in Washington had an appointment to see President Lincoln at five o'clock in the morning. He arrived at a quarter of five and asked to see Mr. Lincoln. The usher said that he would have to wait for fifteen minutes. The visitor waited patiently, when from the next room he heard a voice in very earnest conversation. So he asked, " Who is talking in the next room? " Then the usher explained that it was the President, whose custom it was to read the Bible and to pray from four to five o'clock every morning. You see, Abraham Lincoln had such a firm faith and trust in God that he felt the need of daily Bible reading and prayer. We would do well to follow his example and take as our own motto, " In God We Trust."

Now let us again look at our coin. Two more phrases stand out, *E Pluribus Unum* and " Liberty." The Latin words *e pluribus unum* mean " One out of many." " Liberty " means free, as it is used in the Declaration of Independence, " All men are created free and equal."

What does *e pluribus unum* or " one out of many " mean? Let us look at our hand. We see five fingers but one hand. One finger alone cannot do much, but the hand is the most wonderful tool in the world. One hand made out of five fingers. 'Way back at the beginning of our country there were thirteen colonies made into one nation—*e pluribus unum,* one nation out of many. Just as the five fingers work together to make one hand, so the many states of our country work together to make one strong nation.

But at the time when Abraham Lincoln became President this motto was no longer true. Our country was divided over whether slavery should continue to exist and whether a state had a right to secede from the Union. The Civil War was the result of this controversy. Lincoln believed that all men should be free and equal, that the nation could not exist half free and half slave. Lincoln said, " I know I am right, because I know that liberty is right, for Christ teaches it." At another time he said, " I know the Lord is always on the right side; but God is my witness that it is my constant prayer that both myself and this Nation should be on the Lord's side." One of the results of the Civil War was the freeing of the slaves; also our nation again became one, " one nation indivisible, with liberty and justice for all." Once more we are proud of our mottoes, " Liberty " and *E Pluribus Unum*. They and the other motto, " In God We Trust," are justly found on the same coin with Abraham Lincoln. We can truly say, " In God we trust," if every day, as Abraham Lincoln did, we look to our heavenly Father in prayer.

42

WEARING A MASK

Object: A mask.

Story: In my hand I hold a mask. I am sure many of you have worn a mask to a Hallowe'en party. When you wear a mask you pretend or make believe that you are someone else. When plays were given in ancient times the actors wore masks. If the play called for an old man the actor would wear a mask representing a man who had gray hair and a lined face. In the mask were openings for eyes, nose and mouth through which the actor could see, breathe and with his voice imitate the speech of an old man. Such an actor makes believe. He pretends to be someone else. It is perfectly all right for an actor to make believe or pretend to be what he is not, but when a person does that in daily life to fool people who trust him we call him a hypocrite.

When we wear a mask we make believe. So the hypocrite is a make-believe man. If we wear a mask we have two faces or we are two-faced. A hypocrite, then, is a two-faced man, he is not what he seems to be. I think you would be interested in hearing a definition of the word hypocrite which I read recently: " He. is like new satin outside with a poor lining on the inside." Jesus called the Pharisees hypocrites because they were two-faced. In front of people they made believe that they were very good, but behind their backs they were not what they pretended to be.

We would not wear a mask (hold up mask) like this one all the time, for then we would be two-faced. When we are two-faced we wear one face for ourselves and the other for the world. If we do this continually we soon will not know which one is our real self. The great French actor Coquelin often played the part of Jesus Christ in religious plays. He played this part with so much emotion and intensity that he finally came to the point where he could not see any difference between himself and Jesus Christ. He believed that he actually was Jesus, and at last he lost his mind and had to go to an asylum for the insane.

At Hallowe'en we wear a mask and we have fun in trying to be someone else. But in real life we must not pretend to be what we are not. Then we are hypocrites or deceivers. When we look at this mask we think of two-faced people, of people who pretend to be what they are not. We say to ourselves, " I don't want to be a hypocrite, I want to be myself."

In what way can people be hypocrites, or, in other words, wear a mask? The president of a bank was asked to address the graduating class in a high school. He chose as his topic, " Honesty is the best policy." Several weeks later he disappeared with fifty thousand dollars of the bank's money. He pretended to be honest, he wore a mask, but at heart he was a thief. In other words, he was a hypocrite.

Jesus said that there are people who are like wolves in sheep's clothing. Imagine a wolf putting on the skin of a sheep in order to look like a sheep. This reminds me of a story which you all know, the story of Little Red Riding Hood. This little girl was sent to her grandmother's house with a basket of food. The road led through the woods, where she met a wolf, who stopped and talked to her in a gentle and kindly voice. She told him where she was going. By taking a short cut the wolf arrived there first. He killed and ate the grandmother and when Little Red Riding Hood arrived, he pretended to be her grandmother. Had it not been for some woodsmen who rescued Little Red Riding Hood, the wolf would have killed her too. The wolf pretended to be gentle and kind, but he was planning to kill and eat the little girl. He was a wolf in sheep's clothing, a hypocrite, a deceiver, for he pretended to be the little girl's grandmother, when really he was a bad wolf.

Hypocrites, two-facers and pretenders, do not present a pretty picture. Be your best self. Always be true, honest, loyal, and faithful to God. Do not make believe; do not wear a mask in real life.